The complete book of
DOGS

YVONNE REES

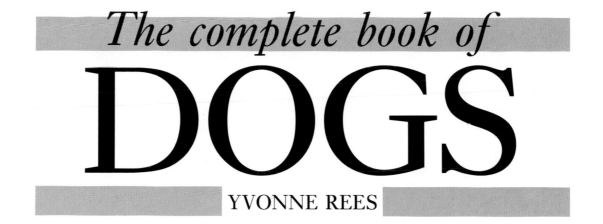

The complete book of
DOGS

YVONNE REES

CRESCENT BOOKS
NEW YORK • AVENEL, NEW JERSEY

CLB 2754
© 1993 Colour Library Books Ltd., Godalming, Surrey, England.
All rights reserved.

This 1993 edition published by Crescent Books,
distributed by Outlet Book Company, Inc.,
a Random House Company
40 Engelhard Avenue, Avenel, New Jersey 07001
Printed and bound in Hong Kong.

ISBN 0 517 06594 0
8 7 6 5 4 3 2 1

The Author

Yvonne Rees is a writer and lecturer on a wide range of
subjects, including wildlife and animals. She shares her home
with a variety of animals, including two cats and two dogs.
Looking after pets for friends has involved Yvonne in keeping
an eye on anything from quails and peacocks to cats, dogs,
goats, hens and sheep. In her spare time Yvonne likes to
paint, often preparing pet portraits for proud owners.

Credits

Edited and designed: Ideas into Print, Vera Rogers and
  Stuart Watkinson
Photographs: Marc Henrie, David Dalton and FLPA
Layouts: Sue Cook   Typesetting: Ideas into Print
Commissioning Editor: Andrew Preston
Production: Ruth Arthur, Sally Connolly, Andrew Whitelaw
Director of Production: Gerald Hughes
Color Separations: Advance Laser Graphic Arts
  (International) Ltd., Hong Kong.

*Above: A pair of Basset Hounds,
immediately endearing with their
doleful expression and lugubrious
bearing. But appearances can be
deceiving, because these dogs are
true hounds that relish plenty of
exercise in the great outdoors.*

*Endpapers: Three delightful
Tibetan Spaniels pose for the
camera. These happy dogs were
first discovered in Tibetan
monastries and make enjoyable pets.*

*Half-title page: A Long-coated
Chihuahua - the smallest of dogs.*

*Title page: An Airedale Terrier -
a loyal and powerful breed.*

Contents

The dog in history

We are not really sure of the true origins of the dog. Did it, for example, evolve directly from the wolves that used to roam widely in what was a rather more hostile environment all those thousands of years ago? When did man first discover that this creature - primarily a pack animal - could be 'domesticated' and become a useful, even invaluable companion? The dog's earliest antecedents probably took many shapes and forms, from small ferretlike mammals to something closely resembling a wolf. Dogs certainly belong to the group that includes wolves, jackals, hyenas and martens, but behavioral and anatomical evidence suggests they are more likely to be descended from the wolf than from any of the others. We know that by 12000BC man was using dogs for hunting and that these animals were

Above: A papyrus painting of about 1250BC shows Anubis, the jackal- or wolf-headed god of the dead worshipped by the Ancient Egyptians, weighing the heart of the deceased against the feather of truth.

quite unmistakably early dogs and not wolves. By the Bronze Age (3500-1000BC) dogs resembling some of today's breeds were being used for hunting and as guard dogs to protect stock from wilder predators. It was during this period that the five distinct dog types evolved to which all today's breeds are related: the spitz, greyhound, pointer, mastiff and sheepdog. Extensive cross-breeding over thousands of years, has created certain types of dog to suit man's purposes, from fierce fearless dogs for fighting to fast-moving animals for sport and hardy biddable breeds as hunting companions. Once man began to travel, as soldier, merchant or explorer, different types of dog also became interbred. Only where a dog was native to a particularly isolated area or region, such as the island-bound Ibizan Hound or the desert Saluki, has a breed stayed true to type for thousands of years. We

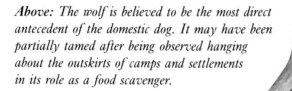

Above: The wolf is believed to be the most direct antecedent of the domestic dog. It may have been partially tamed after being observed hanging about the outskirts of camps and settlements in its role as a food scavenger.

Right: This skull, identified as belonging to one of the earliest domestic dogs, proves that man's hunting companion already had many dog, rather than wolf characteristics.

can trace the dog's association with man back to earliest times, not just through archeological evidence - and a pile of bones may mean the dog was a meal as much as a companion - but more accurately from carvings, paintings and writings that reveal how the dog might have looked and how it was used. In many surviving floor mosaics, for example, we can see that the Romans favored a type of mastiff as a useful hunting and stock dog, as well as a house guard and source of entertainment at the circus. The Ancient Greeks also had their mastiffs and greyhounds - and a mythical three-headed dog, Cerberus, was said to guard the entrance to the Underworld. Dogs frequently feature in religion and mythology. Apart from Cerberus, the best-known example is probably Anubis, the Egyptian god of the dead, although his head on top of a

human body is rather wolflike. Dogs seem to have played a large part in the lives of the Ancient Egyptians. Countless carvings, paintings and statues depict greyhounds, mastiffs and a form of bloodhound, all used as guards, hunters and even pets, although this was a relatively new idea. The dog's role in man's society became increasingly important through history, adapting successfully to sport, work or companionship, from the shepherd's sheepdog to the princess's lapdog.

Left: Equipped only with a leashed, mastiff-type dog and a spear, this Abyssinian hunter's quarry is a lion. This relief from Nineveh dates from 668-622BC.

All shapes and sizes

The range of shapes and sizes within the dog world is truly extraordinary. When you see a huge bearlike Saint Bernard beside a tiny fluffy Pekingese or the almost rodentlike Mexican Hairless, it is hard to believe that their basic anatomy is the same. However, all dogs are descended from five main dog types whose characteristics can be identified in the body shape and behavior of today's dogs. Some breeds have been so extensively refined and crossbred that the clues are hard to find, while others have remained almost completely true to the original 'blueprint'. As well as man's part in producing dogs to suit his purpose, climate and location also mold a particular breed's body type and character. For example, animals that live in cold climates, such as the Husky, have a thicker skin as well as an abundance of hair - often a double coat. Hunting dogs required to cover great distances, such as the Greyhound or Saluki, are built for speed, and even their tails are modified to provide optimum streamlining and balance. You can often spot a spitz type by its stocky body and feathery curled tail. They are mainly snow- and ice-dogs, such as the Samoyed, Akita and Husky, but also include the woolly Chow Chow and tiny Pomeranian. Greyhound roots are also easily identified by a lean, high-stomached physique and narrow head, as seen in the Afghan, Deerhound and Pharaoh Hound. Mountain dogs and mastiffs, such as the Leonberger and Bull Mastiff, are large and muscular, making them good workers and guard dogs. The dog's physical characteristics have been carefully defined and there are long names to describe them. Tall dogs, such as the Great Dane, are said to be hypermetric, medium-sized dogs are eumetric and the tiniest breeds are known as elliptometric. A square or stocky breed is mediolinear; if it has a long body in relation to its height it is brevilinear. The muzzle may be slender and extended like a Collie's or blunt as a Boxer's, and there are many different classifications for the shape of head. Ears may be erect or drooping, and triangle, button- or heart-shaped. The tail may curl up or down and be slim or bushy. A short-, long- or medium- haired coat of a single color is described as self-colored, brindled (with black stripes) or pied (white with colored patches).

When it comes to behavior, common doglike characteristics are easier to identify right across the range of breeds. Essentially, all dogs behave according to their ancient instincts, tempered by what they are taught and the conditions in which they live. The dog is a pack animal and likes company, so it tends to be friendly. Beacuse one of its instincts is to defend its territory, it is loyal and a good guard. Its hunting instinct is strong and more developed in some breeds than in others. Inborn sexual and maternal instincts also influence a dog's behavior. You can relate most of your dog's daily activity to these basic instincts: the sniffing, barking, whining, the aggression or attempts at domination, the expression of its face, attitude of its body and even the action of the tail are all instinctive.

Above: The French Bulldog is small and muscular, but not as fierce as it looks. On the contrary, it is playful and affectionate and enjoys human company.

Right: Chow Chows have the classic spitz shape, but their thick coats make them as cuddly as a teddy bear. Brush the coat every day to keep it in good condition.

Below: A proud smooth-haired Dachshund showing off its curiously elongated body and short legs. This breed is prone to obesity and needs plenty of exercise.

Left: What energy - and what fun these two Standard Poodles are having, as they bound around the garden like a couple of enthusiastic lions. They have been clipped in the traditional lion style, intended to imitate the physical features of those big cats.

Right: Up and over! This Weimaraner has no problem clearing the five-bar gate in its pathway. The strong muscular hindquarters and lithe body shape enable the dog to propel itself easily over such obstacles. They are also useful attributes for hunting big game over rough terrain in its German homeland. As the name suggests, it was originally bred and developed in Weimar, Germany, by crossing hunting dogs belonging to local associates with Bloodhounds and various breeds of Pointers, these two types being the main stock. The Weimaraner is becoming increasingly popular as a pet, because it makes a good guard dog and a friendly companion. If they are looked after and schooled properly, Weimaraners are renowned for being one of the best behaved breeds in the dog world - a characteristic that certain owners are always keen to find in a dog breed.

Right: *Most agile dogs can be trained to perform a variety of different tricks: this particular act is popular among circus animals. Body control and balance, together with good, strong hindquarters are called for to achieve the required position. The smaller the dog, the better it is for this kind of trick, as it is easier for small animals to support their own weight on two legs. Some dogs can perform this trick on the back of a horse as it trots around the circus ring. The flexibility of the back legs and strong muscles enable the dog to stretch out as far as it possibly can, achieving a stance in which the hindlegs are in almost the same position as if it were running at full pace. Strong, well-angled legs are important in any dog, not just to ensure that they look well, but also because any irregularity or disability will affect the animal's general mobility. The legs should look parallel when viewed from front or back, never bandy- or barrel-legged, pigeon-toed, knock-kneed (called cow-hocked) or too widely spread apart (known as hocking out). All the leg joints should meet at the correct angles. This is known as angulation; poor angulation will upset the dog's posture and can occur anywhere on the body, including, the shoulders, wrists, elbows, hocks or stifles. The stifle is the kneelike joint above the heel in the hindleg.*

Left: The English Toy Terrier, also called the Toy Manchester Terrier in North America, is an observant and inquisitive little animal. The ears are long and the tail is very thin, resembling a whip pointed at the end.

Below: The Siberian Husky is the only type of Husky that is officially recognized as a breed under that name. It is an extremely hardy, thickset animal and very popular among sled-racing sportsmen. It is one of the calmest and best-natured of all the sled dogs, which enables it to work very well in a pack. The head is shaped rather like that of a fox, the eyes are either brown or blue or, in this case, one of each. The thick coat comes in many colors and markings.

Left: *The Lowchen is a small but strongly-built dog with a long thin silky coat that comes in a wide range of colors. Traditionally, this was cut to resemble a lion, giving the dog its pet name of 'petit chien lion' meaning 'little lion dog'. However, this cut is not so popular today. The breed is very much a European dog and often features in old oil paintings by artists such as Goya. It has become much more common in the UK since its introduction in the 1970s, but is virtually unknown in the US. It is believed to be related to the small water spaniels and the bichon family of dogs. Lowchens are regularly seen at shows, but seem to be less popular as pets. This seems a shame as they are affectionate, intelligent and very obedient little dogs*

Right: *The sturdy Fox Terrier is traditionally a hunting dog and, as its name suggests, was once a popular breed for fox hunting, particularly in eighteenth century England. There are two different breeds: the smooth- and the wire-haired, but both have the same characteristics and eager, alert manner. They have a stocky, powerful body, with strong, muscular legs – useful attributes in a hunting dog that had to keep up with the hunt and needed plenty of stamina for long hours spent covering rough ground in variable weather conditions. Alert and muscular, these dogs clearly need plenty of exercise and indeed they are not happy unless allowed plenty of access to outdoors. They are lively, but also fairly aggressive and enjoy fighting with other dogs.*

Left: The easily recognizable Pembroke Corgi is a popular pet with a noisy bark and quite capable of standing its ground against intruders. Years ago, these little dogs were used for herding and rounding up cattle on the rolling grasslands in their Welsh homeland.

Below: The Finnish Spitz is sometimes known by its nickname the Barking Bird Dog. It is able to track and flush out game birds into the safety of the trees ahead of its master, and then continues barking to indicate where the birds are hiding out.

Right: The Norfolk Terrier is one of the smallest of the terrier group of dogs today. It resembles the Norwich Terrier, but has dropped ears, whereas those of the Norwich are pointed. It is this characteristic that is used to differentiate between the two varieties.

Below: Surprisingly, perhaps, it is the bigger dogs that are frequently more affectionate and less aggressive than a great many of the smaller breeds. This makes them excellent and lovable pets, providing you can allow them plenty of space to exercise. The Golden Retriever is a very good example of a good all-round family pet. It is an attractive, well-proportioned dog, with a strong well-built body and a thick, sometimes wavy golden or cream-colored coat. This dog's calm, patient nature ensures that it is a good companion for children; its equable temperament combined with an unshakable loyalty towards its owner means that it makes a good family guard dog, too. Old instincts die hard and this is still one of the world's best retrieving dogs, originally trained to retrieve waterfowl - a job it still does very well today. The Golden Retriever certainly shows no hesitation whatsoever when faced with the opportunity to leap into water and fetch for its master. As well as being developed as a fine retrieving dog, this hardy breed is actually a good all-round gundog. It has strong jaws, a highly developed sense of smell and an active nature. Being intelligent, this is also a dog that responds well to training, loving nothing better than to please his or her owner. This picture shows four adult dogs.

Above: A dog's sense of smell is very highly developed and it plays an important part in the animal's everyday instinctive behavior, especially in relation to other dogs. As well as leading the dog eagerly into the undergrowth on the scent trail of a rabbit or small rodent, its nose also tells it a great deal about the activities of its fellow canines. You must have noticed how all dogs give each other a good sniff all over when they meet – this is for identification purposes. Dogs leave olfactory messages around the garden and on street corners, too; scratching and urinating leaves a urinary and glandular message.

Right: The elegant Saluki relies less on its sense of smell for hunting than on its extremely sharp eyesight. The dog's natural habitat is the desert, where it once used the superb speed of its long, muscular legs to course hare, fox and gazelle. A few Arab tribes still hunt with falcon and saluki, carrying them behind the saddle to protect their paws from the scorching sand. Modern Arabs keep Salukis mainly for ceremonial hunting and, although the dogs are extremely hardy – being tolerant of both extreme heat and a limited water supply – they are usually transported by horse or motor vehicle.

Left: The Chihuahua is believed to be the smallest dog in the world and instantly recognizable – although it can be hard to spot underfoot being only 6–8in(15–20cm) high. There is a longhaired type, but this is the smooth-coated variety, with a thick glossy coat, the familiar large, erect ears and the tail curved over the back. Although the dog is small, it should not be carried around too much as it needs a fair amount of exercise. The Chihuahua is loyal and playful with its owner, but can be quick-tempered with strangers or if it feels it is not getting enough attention.

Below: The Dalmatian is best known for its good looks and handsome spotted coat, making it more like a fashion accessory over the centuries.

Right: Despite its fighting past, the Bulldog is a quiet complacent pet, well suited to family life providing it is well trained. Perhaps as it snoozes contentedly, it dreams of the days when its ancestors pitched themselves against some quite formidable opponents including, as its name suggests, bulls. Bull baiting was a popular spectacle that was eventually abolished in 1835. The plucky Bulldog was also once pitched against bears, badgers and even other Bulldogs. Its fighting strength lies partly in the powerful jaws that can lock together like a vice. The dog's thickset barrel-like body stands square on short, muscular legs, and the large broad head of this former fighter has a short snub-nosed muzzle and heavy jowels, the skin hanging in wrinkled folds.

Choosing a dog

Before acquiring a dog, there are several factors that you should consider, especially if you have no previous experience of keeping one. Never make a hasty decision; take time to assess exactly what you want from your new companion and what you are able to offer in return. The choice of dogs available today is tremendous - not only the registered breeds, but also the many thousands of mongrels and crossbreds. Many people take a liking to a certain breed and decide that it is the one for them without giving any thought to the practical implications. Some dogs, for example, can live as long as 18 years, and require a considerable amount of care later in life, so look on owning a dog as a long-term commitment. Many long-haired breeds need a great deal of grooming and clipping; they shed their coats and leave hairs that need to be cleared up. Large, active dogs require plenty of feeding and exercise. Even some of the smaller dogs need a lot of exercise. How much time can you devote to your pet? Think carefully before buying a dog as a gift for someone else. Do you know how much they are prepared to take on? It would be dreadful if an elderly person was burdened with a dog they could not cope with and it became aggressive through neglect or had to be put down. Owning a dog is a serious business. Like most domesticated animals, it will become a member of the family and needs to feel secure and cared for. In return for its keep and your companionship, a dog will offer affection, loyalty and protection, depending on breed type. Your home and lifestyle will be a great influence on the kind of dog you choose. Some breeds are better suited than others to the confined life of an apartment owner; others are so large you will need a very spacious home or a kennel outside. There are dogs that retain their puppy playfulness until they are quite elderly. This can be very amusing until you approach old age yourself and would prefer a more sedate companion. Young children in the home should also influence your choice of dog. There is always the chance of an accident with any dog. Even a gentle breed may turn nasty if it feels its territory is being invaded or it is hurt accidentally in a tender place, such as the ears. Never consider one of the more aggressive breeds trained as a guard. Generally speaking, bigger dogs tend to be more placid, while the miniature breeds are less equable and require more care.

Above: It is important that all members of the family should be prepared for the responsibilities involved in owning a dog and learn how to look after it.

Left: No matter how old the owner, a dog will bring immense enjoyment and satisfaction. Here, a devoted pet waits patiently for its master to pat and stroke it.

Right: Only a real dog lover would consider sharing their home with several dogs, however appealing the breed. Apart from the work involved in grooming and exercising, there is the cost of feeding and keeping them healthy.

Left: When you have decided that the time is right, calmly introduce a new member of the family to your pet dog. Never leave a young child unattended with a dog, especially one that it is unfamiliar with. It will take quite a while before your pet understands fully that the newcomer does not pose a threat to it.

Below: Providing that your children are accustomed to dogs, and understand that they must never treat them roughly, there is absolutely no reason why they should not be able to play happily together. However, a tranquil scene could easily turn to disaster should the dogs turn on them unexpectedly and all young children need to be taught to be aware of this possibility.

Above: These twins and their pet Golden Retriever are enjoying a walk with mother. As you can see, the dog is fully under control and needs hardly any restraint. This is very important, particularly in traffic. It not only makes life a lot easier if you are not being towed along by your animal, but once it has been taught this level of control it should not be any trouble to lead.

Right: Some dogs absolutely love the water while others refuse to go near it whatever the inducement. This Bull Mastiff obviously loves to get thoroughly wet and needs little encouragement to splash about. Given plenty of exercise and stimulating play, dogs will be more content and easier to control, not to mention the fun they derive from these activities. Their owner should enjoy these outings too.

Left: There are various clubs and societies throughout the world to which people can take their dogs. At the meetings, owners can discuss any behavioral problems with professional handlers and learn various control techniques.

Choosing a dog

Below left: The more space a dog has to run around in the better, especially one that needs plenty of exercise, such as these American Cocker Spaniels enjoying themselves among the bluebells. Apart from a regular walk, your dog will enjoy a little freedom off the lead every now and then, even if it is only for a short time. This chance to let its hair down will prevent it from getting bored at home and also uses up plenty of surplus energy. Just like their owners, dogs soon get out of condition, and a leisurely stroll does not exert them to the full. Most responsible dog owners take the time and trouble to give their dogs the chance of fresh air and a good romp in the park or open countryside whenever they can.

Below: Airedales are great fun-lovers and providing they are given a firm hand from a very early age and plenty of regular exercise, they make entertaining pets. However, their wiry black-and-tan coats do need regular attention, otherwise the dogs look more like shaggy bears. Being rough and thick, the coat should be regularly groomed and professionally clipped - never try to do this yourself with ordinary clippers as they will cut the hair too close.

Right: A dog breeder and her Golden Retrievers. Not everyone is lucky enough to have access to this much land and open space – you can see how much the dogs are enjoying it. Their owner is using a whistle to keep them under control as they bound about joyously, twisting and turning or stopping from time to time to explore the new or strange scents they may encounter. Most dog breeders will tell you if their breed has any special requirements or likely drawbacks and this will help you to find the right type of dog for your particular lifestyle. Retrievers such as those shown here, for example, need a home with enthusiastic active owners, where they will be assured of plenty of exercise. Without this, they will tend to put on fat and their muscles and joints will stiffen up.

Right: Traditionally, Siberian Huskies are working sled dogs, famed for their speed and endurance. These handsome dogs are becoming increasingly popular, particularly in North America, where they have distinguished themselves in the sport of dog sled racing by collecting several world titles. The pack instinct is strong and the dogs make a good team, rarely quarreling among themselves. The Siberian Husky is a clean dog with no 'doggy' odor and many are kept for show or sport. There are many colors, including white, and some dogs have distinctive head markings. Its close relationship with the wolf means that despite being affectionate and good-natured, it must be handled with sensitivity and patience in order not to arouse its anger.

Right: All dogs must be taught to walk obediently, both on and off the leash, to ensure that an enjoyable walk does not turn out to be a battle of wills between the animal and yourself. Training begins on the leash and progresses to a long rope about 10ft(3m) long. A rope measuring about 15ft(4.5m) fools the dog into thinking it is free and is used to teach it to come to heel. If the dog does not respond to the command, tug sharply on the rope, but never move towards the dog before it reaches you.

Below: A dog may be taught to sit, stay and lie using the leash. Initially, the leash is used to control the dog's head while you use your free hand to reinforce the command - say by pressing down on the dog's back or hindquarters. These are Maremma Sheepdogs.

Left: The Basset Hound is one of the most popular pet breeds – but surely not because of its good looks. The Basset's barrel-like body is carried so low on short solid legs that its belly almost seems to scrape the ground; the skin is loosely folded and the eyes irresistibly doleful. No, most people choose a Basset because they make such excellent dog companions. Loyal and affectionate, the Basset Hound is calm and gentle, generally well behaved and never boisterous. That does not mean to say that this breed does not need much exercise. The Basset may look like a real couch potato, but this former hunting dog needs regular access to open ground, where it will prove itself surprisingly agile and very eager to wander off.

Right: Essentially a sporting dog, the Weimaraner is often chosen as a pet because it is so attractive. It has a powerful but well-proportioned body and an elegantly shaped head with amber eyes. But it is the coat that attracts most attention and admiration: it looks like soft suede in a wonderful shade of silvery or fawn gray and needs very little grooming. The Weimaraner will also make an enjoyable pet, providing it is handled firmly and strictly trained from an early age, otherwise you may well find that the dog proves wayward. It could also be difficult and destructive if confined indoors without adequate exercise. The animal is extremely active and requires long and regular periods of exercise to keep it fit and contented. If it is correctly trained, it makes a very good guard dog, although it is not a vicious breed. It can also be one of the best-behaved breeds, often appearing in obedience competitions. It must be strong and fearless too, for in its native Germany the Weimaraner was originally bred for big game hunting and later became a popular bird dog and water retriever. The dog was originally developed in Weimar, Germany, by crossing bloodhounds with different pointers to produce an excellent all-round hunting dog. It owes its name to one of the Grand Dukes of Weimar, who developed the breed for hunting at the end of the eighteenth century and originally kept it for his exclusive use in order to keep the breed pure.

Left: Like most large dogs, the massive Saint Bernard is extremely calm and good natured so makes an excellent family pet for those who have space to keep it and the time and energy to give this lively dog regular vigorous exercise and a weekly grooming. Weighing up to 132lb (60kg) and standing maybe 25-27in (65-70cm) tall with its huge shaggy bearlike head and long thick coat, the Saint Bernard is gentle as a lamb and can be trusted never to get flustered or annoyed by young children. It is almost part of folklore how the breed made its name as a vital member of the alpine rescue service, where its excellent sense of smell and sure-footedness have helped rescue so many people lost in the snow over the last couple of hundred years. This breed has proved to be intelligent and easy to train.

A puppy in the home

Female dogs become sexually receptive about every six months and are described as being 'in heat'. They become restless, and the chemicals secreted in their urine attract male dogs from a considerable distance. This can be a nuisance, so unless you intend to breed from your bitch, consider having her neutered. Male dogs with no access to a bitch may become frustrated and aggressive and it may be advisable to have them castrated. When a bitch whelps (i.e. produces her pups), the procedure follows that of any dog in the wild. A few days before the event, she will choose a private place in which to give birth and once the pups are born, she licks them to stimulate their natural functions. The mother will become aggressive if she feels that anyone is threatening her pups and it is best not to disturb her too much. When she feels safe, she will allow members of the family to touch the pups for short periods of time. She generally looks after her litter well: if a puppy yelps in distress, she will seek it out and fetch it back by the scruff of the neck. A gentle lick reassures it and keeps it clean, while a quick nip teaches it to behave. The bitch will be totally responsible for the welfare and education of her pups until they are fully weaned. After about four weeks she may begin to regurgitate half-digested food for them. At about six weeks, the puppies will be weaned and she will begin to leave them to their own devices for longer periods. She no longer fusses over them as much as before and when they try to suckle she may give them a bite to deter them. Taking the litter away too soon or too suddenly could cause the bitch to become ill.

Eclampsia, or convulsions, can result from such premature separation. It is a good idea to leave the mother with at least two of the pups; if this is not possible, remove all the pups together when the time comes and not one at a time.

Be prepared to devote a fair amount of time to a pup once it is weaned. In many ways, keeping two pups is easier, because a single pup tends to become bored and mischievous. Until it is familiar with its surroundings, a young dog in a new house may yap a lot and go off its food. Regular feeding and plenty of attention are essential to help pups settle in well. Provide the dog with a place to sleep - a cushion, basket or blanket - and try not to keep moving its position. A few toys will help keep it amused, but anything chewable will have to be moved out of reach, especially at night, when a solitary pup gets lonely or bored. A good diet is vital; check what is recommended for your breed. Small, frequent meals should ensure steady growth. Exercise and play are equally important for the pup's development, both physical and mental. If possible, take the dog outside to experience new sights and smells and to enjoy the fresh air. Toilet training should start as soon as possible, but be prepared to be patient and do not expect results too soon.

Right: A proud family of Hovawarts, an old German breed, with their successfully weaned pups.

Left: These German Shepherd puppies look cuddly, but will grow into fierce, efficient guard dogs, if given a firm hand.

Left: A young Golden Retriever puppy. Sometimes you may need a place to keep your pup out of harm or somewhere for it to recover from illness. A pen such as this will restrain it and prevent it from damaging your furniture.

Below: Who would ever believe that these four cute Italian Greyhound pups will one day be capable of racing at up to 40mph (64kph)? They make an ideal pet - although not for running after - as they are small and quiet. They like to play and adore sleeping in front of a nice warm fireplace. However, their gentle nervous nature does not make them suitable as guard dogs.

Left: A Bearded Collie and her pup. With its long shaggy coat, the breed resembles an Old English Sheepdog. Like all Collie breeds, these dogs can be extremely affectionate to their master and family.

Above: A King Charles Spaniel and her puppies just before the weaning stage. Now that the pups have reached this age they no longer depend entirely on their mother for food, and you should offer them an additional feed that they can easily digest. Most bitches will not tolerate the pups pestering her for milk all the time, and the older they get, the more they demand. If there is not much milk available they can become very aggressive, biting and scratching at the teats and causing the mother to snap or even hide away out of reach in a bid to prevent the pups from suckling any longer. Make sure that the mother has plenty of food and water to enable her to feed all her puppies.

Left: Not all puppies are lucky enough to be fed by their mothers. Animal welfare groups are often faced with this problem, as there is a small minority of uncaring people who abandon puppies in cardboard boxes or sacks outside the sanctuaries of these organizations. Throughout the day and night, the staff offer the puppy frequent feeds of milk in small amounts. This continues until the pup reaches weaning age - usually no later than about twelve weeks - or until it is able to cope with other forms of food.

Above: *Two sleepy Labrador pups. As well as needing plenty of excercise, it is important for the developing puppies to have plenty of sleep. After watching them run about all morning, getting in and out of mischief, it can be quite amusing to see them crash out in the most unlikely places. A companion of their own age is ideal and keeps them happy and contented while asleep and at play – a puppy on its own tends to get bored and lonely, which can lead to naughtiness.*

Left: *All pups look cute and none more so than this Westie, or West Highland White Terrier, which will not grow to much more than 11in(28cm) high. These lively little dogs are the result of carefully controlled interbreeding involving other small rough-haired terriers, such as Scotties and Cairns. They were specifically bred as hunting animals, intended to keep down the numbers of foxes and otters. This is why their coats are always pure white; it distinguishes them from their quarry when out hunting.*

Above: A puppy, such as this English Springer Spaniel, can make a fine friend for a young child. Helping to care for the animal, perhaps by feeding, grooming and playing with it, teaches the youngster a useful sense of responsibility.

Right: These Chow Chow pups are no doubt destined to become loyal household pets, but they were once hard-working hunting dogs in China and even a Cantonese delicacy, farm-reared and eaten at about nine months old.

Above: Here's an armful - a litter of Pharaoh Hound pups, an ancient hound breed that has changed little since its ancestors were chosen to decorate Egyptian tombs. Despite its slender elegance, these dogs are very hardy.

Right: Children should be shown how to handle a young dog correctly and taught not treat it as a toy to be casually lifted and awkwardly carried. Unless the puppy is properly supported, it may suffer an injury or even turn nasty.

Left: Early training is essential if your dog is to grow up well behaved and obedient; about three months old is not too young to start. You will need plenty of patience to repeat the same command over and over again until it is understood, but hard work now is amply rewarded later on. A lively or dominant dog will not be easy to discipline if you have not started some sort of training program by the time it is six months old. House training is equally important and can also start at three months by taking the pup outside six or eight times a day. Again, be patient, as the lesson may be long in the learning.

Below: The distinctively ugly profile of the British Bulldog is a result of selective breeding over the last century, using natural mutations of dogs that probably once looked more like the Staffordshire Bull Terrier. The animal has a huge head on a thickset, muscular body, and a squashed-in face that has made it prone to breathing problems and drooling. Its antecedents may have earned their name by baiting bulls and hunting wild boar, but the modern Bulldog has had all the aggressiveness bred out and is a good-natured, loyal pet.

Right: See how a mother's characteristics can be passed directly and virtually unchanged to her offspring. This Borzoi is understandbly proud of her child. Both are enjoying the fresh air and exercise necessary for the good health of both a mother and young dog. Bitches are generally good mothers, taking care of all their pups' needs until they are fully weaned. A strong bond is forged between the mother and her pups from an early age and they clearly enjoy each other's company. Usually it is advisable to leave the bitch with at least two pups or she pines. Even so, when the time comes to remove the litter she may suffer considerably, even to the point of having convulsions. Unless you intend to keep some of the pups, it is a good idea to remove them as as soon as possible after weaning.

Left: Play is extremely important in a puppy's development, encouraging it to discover new tastes, sights and smells, and preparing it for typical adult dog behavior, such as stalking, guarding and chasing. If your puppy can play with other pups of its own age, or even with young children in the household, it will enjoy its play sessions all the more. This activity also teaches it to interact with other individuals and so develop the appropriate social behavior required as an adult. Even at four to five weeks old, puppies will display classic group behavior and play chasing and prowling games. These Norfolk Terriers are typical of their breed. They are already lively but not overboisterous and will no doubt grow into enjoyable companions or reliable guard dogs, being fearless but not quarrelsome. They are popular among terrier owners, who prefer them for their close, wiry coat that needs very little grooming or regular trimming. These compact, hardy dogs enjoy living in either the town or country, providing they get plenty of exercise.

Above: A Brittany Spaniel pup at seven weeks old. By this stage, you should have started offering it solid foods, as the mother will no longer be able to nourish it entirely with her milk. The upbringing of this small puppy will depend largely on whether you intend to keep it simply as a devoted pet or for the purpose it was originally bred for, namely as a gundog. This breed of spaniel is the fastest of its kind and is particularly suitable for chasing and hunting game on the open moorlands, but also rugged enough to tackle its quarry in rough, bushy and dense undergrowth.

Right: Pups can always be guaranteed to tug at the heartstrings, but these long-haired Dachshunds are especially appealing. As fully grown dogs - and these will not grow very large, having only short legs to support their plump sausage bodies - they make excellent companions, being good-natured and affectionate, although the Dachshund can also be quite mischievous. The longhaired variety is particularly attractive and popular as a pet, despite the extra grooming involved. The long silky coat is available in red, black and tan color combinations.

Caring for your dog

The legendary companionship betwen man and dog is based on mutual trust and affection. Your dog should be confident that it will receive the care it requires and in return will be loyal and obedient. No one likes to see an animal miserable or in poor general condition, let alone one you have grown to love. Correct diet and exercise are vital to good health and it is your responsibility to find out exacly what is required for your particular breed and supply it accordingly. Overfeeding or lack of exercise lead to obesity and boredom. Lack of the right foods will cause your dog to lose condition and eventually become thin and listless. There are many proprietary dog foods on the market that promise a well-balanced diet for particular breeds. You will find instructions on the packaging that help you to work out exactly how much food to offer the dog according to its weight and size. Some foods contain everything the dog needs, while others have to be supplemented with other products. Whether you use canned, dried or fresh foods will depend on what is most convenient for you and on your dog's preference. Dried foods must be accompanied by fresh water at all times. Should you wish to substitute one type of food for another, do so gradually so that the dog's digestive system can slowly adapt. Big, active dogs obviously need more food and a higher level of calcium than medium-sized and small dogs to maintain a healthy coat and strong teeth and bones. You will soon find out what suits your dog best by its general condition. The coat should be glossy and shiny, the nose will be moist and the eyes bright.

Exercise depends very much on the type of dog you own, and although the big dogs clearly need plenty, some of the smaller breeds are also surprisingly active and may need one or two long walks a day. Ideally, a dog should have plenty of space at home to run about in, but if this is not possible, try to find a local park or open ground at a convenient distance from your home. Some shorthaired pedigree dogs are susceptible to colds and must not be allowed to get too cold or damp on such excursions. Dry them thoroughly on your return home. Adequate exercise not only keeps muscles and joints supple, but also prevents the dog becoming bored and restless.

Many dogs require regular grooming or their coats soon begin to look matted and unkempt. A good brushing also helps remove thorns and parasites, and if you neglect this essential task it could be difficult to restore the coat to a good condition. This is particularly true of the longhaired breeds. Their coats are not only more likely to get dirty and tangled, but will also require regular clipping. Depending on the breed, clipping might be a simple job that you can do yourself at home. However, if the dog is to look true to breed type you may need professional help, and the job may require several specialist tools to cope with trimming various parts of the coat to different lengths and finishes. The underside should be equally well groomed. Usually this becomes much dirtier than the top coat, as it collects all the mud and grime, especially in the shorter-legged breeds. Sometimes a sharp object becomes caught in the fur. The dog will scratch vigorously in an effort to extract the object, which may be difficult if it is lodged between the front legs, and the area becomes infected. Prompt action is required as scratching makes the problem worse. The best way to avoid unnecessary suffering is to check for foreign objects caught in the hair when you groom the dog. Remove them carefully, using a sharp knife if necessary.

Right: Regular grooming is an important part of caring for a dog, such as this West Highland White Terrier. It may require professional trimming to conform to breed type or prevent it looking too bushy.

Below: Combing the hair vigorously in the direction that the coat naturally grows is essential when the dog is shedding. It massages the skin and stimulates new growth.

Above: Dobermann puppies feeding from the same dish. Like many short-coated dogs, this breed can be prone to intestinal problems, but these can largely be avoided by making sure the animal does not get chilled when taking exercise in cold weather. Another aid to digestion is a thorough, vigorous daily brushing, which is both soothing and stimulating. Dobermann puppies are also prone to certain skin complaints, so keep your eyes open for bald patches. When three dogs feed from one dish or bowl, you may find that the growth rate of one puppy, such as the middle one shown here, begins to slow down compared with its siblings. This is because the others have become dominant and are taking more food for themselves, while the 'runt', or smallest dog, is not bothering to fight for its share. If this should happen, introduce separate food dishes for each dog and put them down some distance apart.

Right: *At some stage in their life, all dogs chew objects that they are not supposed to, such as your favorite furniture or the odd shoe or two - usually the newest or most expensive pair you own. Young dogs and puppies, being more playful, are the worst culprits as they get bored so easily. A dog that is used to going for walks and running around and fetching sticks will spend hours amusing itself with a lump of wood, tossing it in the air and catching it, biting and chewing it. The Weimaraner pictured here is doing just that. Older dogs should grow out of furniture chewing; if not, they will have to be restrained.*

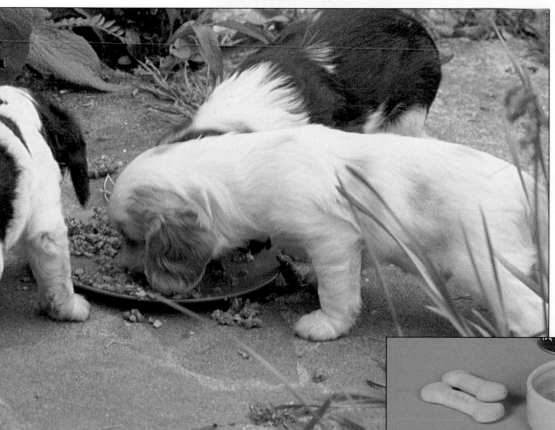

Left: *Cavalier King Charles Spaniels feeding. Although these dogs are small, they require a great deal of attention. Once a brave hunting dog, it still needs plenty of exercise, and the long, silky, well-feathered coat needs daily grooming with a brush and comb. Wipe the eyes gently. The long feathery ears also need regular cleaning with a cotton wad soaked in mild soapy water. Remove any matted hair. These dogs are susceptible to canker in the ears, which causes an unpleasant smell.*

Below: *There are a great many different foodstuffs available today, all specially formulated for dogs. These might vary from simple dog chews to canned products, dry and moist biscuits, meat-flavored chunks and complete dry mixes. Providing the dog is given a well-balanced diet, the type of food you choose will depend on your budget and what is most convenient for you. Commercial foods generally include a selection of added vitamins to compensate for those that are lost during processing.*

Left: It is not always possible to take your pet with you when you go away on business or travel abroad. Unless it is practical for friends, family or neighbors to give your dog the food, exercise and attention it is used to, it is best to find a reputable boarding kennel for it. This should not be too far from your home so that the journey is not traumatic – especially for an animal that is not accustomed to traveling. Unless they are personally recommended, visit the kennels first and make sure they are well maintained. Many provide a particular diet and other special conditions to make your dog feel at home.

Right: As well as the usual walk round town or through the park on a lead, a dog such as this Golden Retriever will appreciate the chance to run and jump in a spacious outdoor area, across a field or on the hills, free of any restraint. This not only helps burn off any surplus energy, making the dog more settled at the end of the day, but also keeps muscles, heart and lungs in trim. If you wish to teach a dog to jump over obstacles, start by encouraging it to clear a low fence or log. Keep the dog on the lead and encourage it to jump by patting the top of the obstacle. Praise the dog as it learns the lesson.

Left: Given the opportunity, accompanying your dog on horseback is a wonderful way for both of you to exercise – and you can keep up without getting tired. However, your dog must be sufficiently well trained to stay under control and to remain close enough to obey essential verbal commands. These Samoyeds are clearly enjoying their run.

Above: Golden Retrievers receiving training. Notice how the two dogs on the floor are waiting patiently while the third is taught how to retrieve an object. Young dogs learn a great deal simply by watching other dogs go through their paces. A more experienced animal – often their own mother – may be used as an example to the others. Only attempt to school one dog at a time; the others must learn to wait quietly for their turn. Should they move or bark, cease the training immediately until they are back under control. Having several dogs to train can be a most enjoyable experience, providing they sit obediently. Eventually you will have the satisfaction of seeing them work in harmony.

Above: Some dogs, particularly traditional working dogs, are easily trained to walk to heel, as generations of following close behind sheep or cattle have been bred into them. There is nothing worse than a dog running uncontrollably in front of you or getting underneath your legs and tripping you up. Introduce the lead while out walking and give the 'heel' command when the dog starts to overtake you, pulling it back each time. When the dog has become used to the idea, try walking down a narrow alley, making sure the dog does not get in front of the lead.

Left: *There are several basic skills that you should teach your dog in order to gain some control over it, otherwise it can pose a problem for you and other people. Once you are satisfied that the dog will not run off, tell it to sit and stay. Then walk a short distance away and call it to come to you. Remember to praise your dog when it behaves well.*

Below: *Whenever you are about to go for a walk with your dog, make sure that it sits quietly while you attach the lead to the collar. The same rule should apply when you are ready to release the dog so it can exercise freely in an open space. Command the dog to sit when you put it on the lead. A well-trained dog should do this straight away.*

Below: Some breeds require professional grooming to keep them looking smart and true to breed type, and they may be traditionally clipped in one of several standard cuts. Originally, the Poodle was trimmed to suit its role as a sporting dog. A shorter coat enabled it to swim more easily, while those areas of the body liable to get cold were left long. Today, the clip is purely cosmetic, and different styles go in and out of fashion. These apricot Poodles have been given a Town and Country cut, currently very popular. The feet and muzzle are closely clipped, leaving long hair on the legs and sometimes whiskers around the mouth. The back, belly, neck and chest are close-shaven. The head is also clipped, leaving a topknot. Pompons on the ankles are optional. You may also sometimes see the Lion clip, which is designed to show off the dog's shape. The hindquarters and hindlegs are shaved bare but leaving showy bracelets around the ankles. The shaved forelegs are given bracelets to match and the lower part of the tail is also shaved, leaving a pompon at the tip.

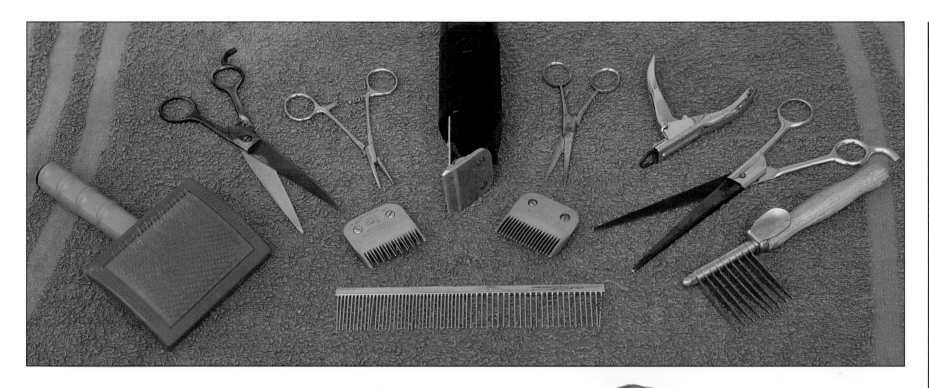

Below: Many of the small lapdogs with their long silky hair require a great deal of attention in proportion to their size. The Lhasa Apso is tiny, almost hidden behind a cascade of hair that has to be brushed, combed and untangled every day. Remove any dirt by dry shampooing with powdered chalk, talcum, or a proprietary dry shampoo for pets. Simply rub it into the coat and brush out thoroughly. These dogs should not have a water bath more than three times a year.

Above: There is a huge choice of grooming equipment for dogs, but usually just a few items are enough to cope with regular cleaning and grooming. As well as a choice of brushes, there are several types of comb to cope with different coats: the standard wide-toothed one is suitable for most normal hair types. A fine-toothed comb is ideal for getting knots out of the coat and a curry comb is normally used for longhaired breeds. Clippers cut the hair very short to give a smooth, sleek appearance. Pointed scissors are used for trimming coarse, thick hair and blunt-tipped ones for thinning out the coat, as these are less likely to snag. For a close finish, use a stripping knife.

Below: A grooming parlor for dogs will be equipped with a wide range of tools to cope with the elaborate cuts that are a feature of certain breeds, such as the Poodle. Owners of show dogs, in particular, have to spend a tremendous amount of time on their dog's appearance if the animal is to conform to the exacting demands of the judges. In other cases, grooming is designed more for the dog's comfort and safety, as well as keeping the coat healthy.

Below: The eyes of a dog are equally important – and just as sensitive to being touched – as our own. They must be gently cleaned at least once a week or even more frequently if they get dirty quickly. If you are washing the eyes yourself, always use a soft piece of cloth or preferably, a swab of absorbent cotton dipped in sterilized water. Regular bathing will remove everyday discharges, often visible at the corners of the eyes. If not removed, these may harden.

Dogs may suffer from a range of eye problems, some of which can seriously affect their sight. One of these is cataracts, which sometimes occur in young dogs but are much more common in older animals. Your dog may simply develop the complaint with age, but it may also be a genetic problem passed down from the dog's parents. What happens is that the eye lens or cornea becomes hard and turns a smoky color, with the result that the dog's vision is severely impaired or it may not be able to see at all. The complaint can affect just one of the eyes, or both at the same time. However, it is possible for a veterinarian to operate on the eye or eyes, to remove the cataracts successfully and restore vision.

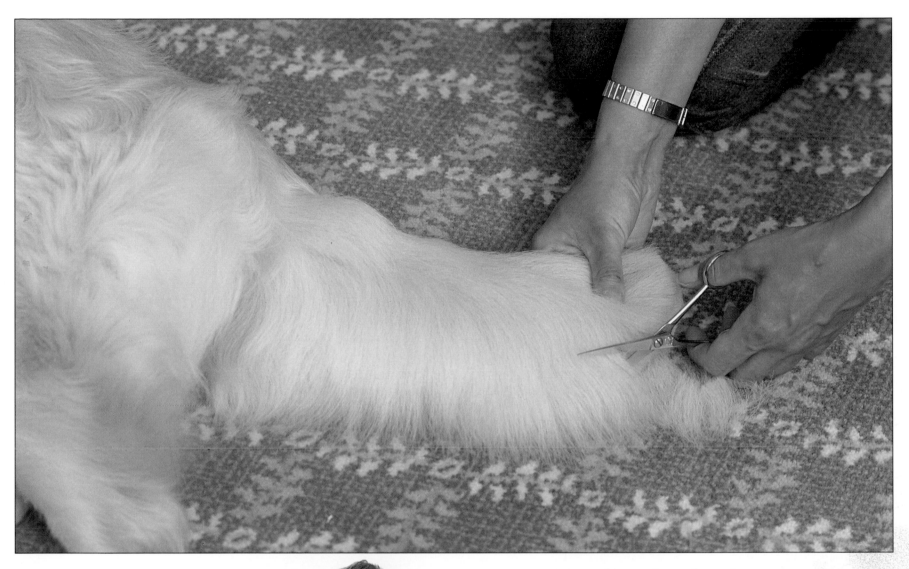

Above: *In some dogs, the tail can become extremely thick and matted, which makes it look out of proportion with the rest of the body. Using a sharp pair of scissors, you should soon be able to remedy the situation. First make sure the dog is relaxed and standing naturally so you can see where to thin the fur. Cut away the unwanted long hair and carefully remove knots and tangles. Take care not to cut too much or make the tail look lopsided. Trim a little hair at a time and then stand back to look at the result. Some dogs resent having anything done to their hindquarters so you may need someone to help you by restraining the animal.*

Below: *The ears of some dogs, such as this Cocker Spaniel, can become matted. Do not pull at any tangles or use force in any way as the ears are tender. A gentle stroking action is normally all that is needed to smooth and brush them.*

Health and safety

No one wants to put their pet at risk and although the majority of dogs seem tough enough to look after themselves, it is your responsibility to ensure their general well-being and to take certain precautions to keep them fit and healthy. This includes taking your dog to the veterinarian for those vital routine inoculations. Some breeds are susceptible to certain ailments and require special attention. Ears and eyes are the most likely areas at risk and need regular and gentle cleaning in all breeds. However, dogs with long floppy ears are especially prone to infection, while many of the selectively bred types must be checked for runny eyes and other signs of eye trouble. Knowing your dog's particular weakness will help you to anticipate any potential problems before they develop. Always contact your veterinarian at the first signs of trouble. In the home, dogs - especially young dogs - should be treated like small children when it comes to protecting them from objects such as plastic bags, medicines, poisonous substances and sharp objects. Always keep these items out of reach. Cans with sharp-edged lids are a common cause of lacerations of the mouth and tongue when a dog attempts to reach the food at the bottom of the container. Unless you can take immediate action after the animal has eaten them, poisons very often cause a fatal reaction. Sometimes a dog may come across baited meat intended to kill vermin. If your dog reacts strangely shortly after it has been for a run in open country, either vomiting vigorously, whining or dragging its legs, the chances are it has consumed something poisonous. Consult a veterinarian at once. If the animal has been sick and you have no idea what it has eaten, put a small amount of the substance in a clean container or plastic bag so that the veterinarian can analyze it before prescribing a specific antidote or remedy. Some dogs, particularly terriers, love to dig and scratch after rabbits, rats and other forms of vermin, usually at the entrance to the hole or burrow where the quarry is seeking refuge. This behavior makes them susceptible to ripping their claws, which can be very painful, but you only become aware of the injury some time later, when the animal starts to limp. If the claw is not too badly ripped and has not become infected, clean and bandage it until it has healed. Keep the dog indoors until it is fully recovered. If it is seriously injured, the claw will have to be removed and this minor operation is carried out under anesthetic. Once the dog has recovered, it will still be able to scratch at holes, so it is a good idea to prevent it from doing so whenever you can.

Above: If it is likely to snap or snarl, it might be a good idea to prevent your dog from biting anyone by ensuring that it is muzzled while you are out among people and other animals. It does not harm the dog, but helps to teach it restraint.

Left: Before you embark on a journey, it is important to ensure that your dogs will be safe while traveling in the rear of the car. A specially made metal cage will prevent them from climbing over the seats. These two Shetland Sheepdogs are ready for their trip.

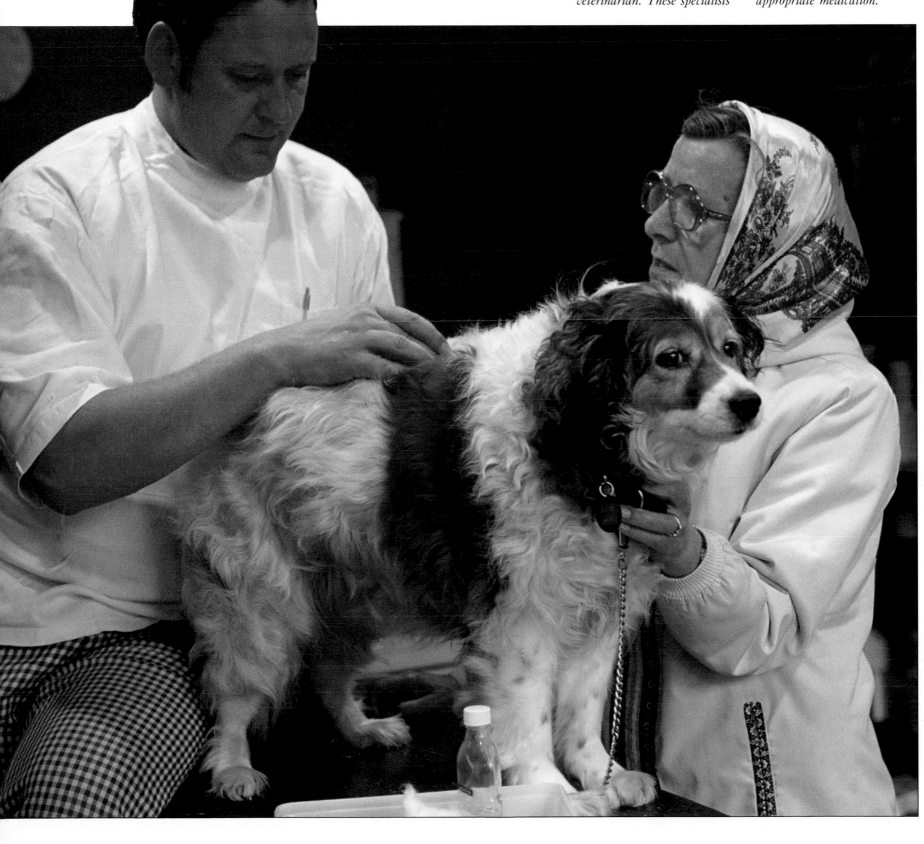

Right: By using a stethoscope, it is possible for a trained person to tell whether or not your dog has any heart or lung problems. As your dog becomes older, these internal organs and tissues will begin to become less reliable. Your verterinarian will advise you on the best treatment for such conditions should they begin to show. As with humans, obesity in dogs can lead to heart failure, and so you may be given dietary advice and recommended levels of exercise. The right food and general fitness will give your dog the best chance of a long, healthy life within its natural span.

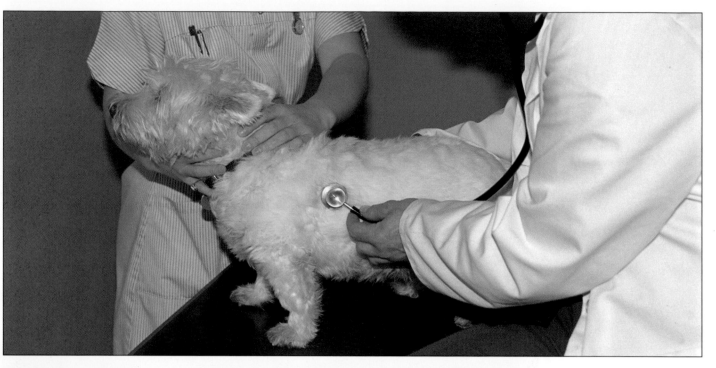

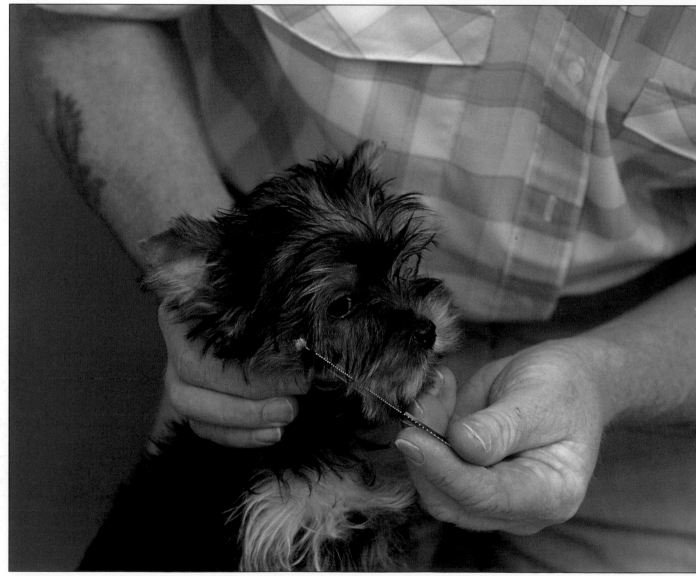

Left: A dog's ears are particularly susceptible to a variety of different infections and diseases, referred to under the general name of otitis. Some breeds are especially prone to trouble: this Yorkshire Terrier will need its ears routinely cleaned with a cotton swab. Your veterinarian will first examine the dog's ear with an instrument known as an otoscope. If he is unsure exactly what the trouble is he will take a minute scraping of the infectious bacteria and test it to find out the most suitable antibiotic with which to treat it. The Spaniel family are prone to ear problems because the inside of the ear is permanently warm and damp, making this area a haven for breeding bacteria, viruses and parasites. A regular wash using absorbent cotton soaked lightly in water is the best routine treatment. Gently rubbing the region immediately inside the ear – never probe deeply – will help to prevent a buildup of wax and germs that could cause problems.

Below: Sometimes it is necessary for your dog to go to the veterinary clinic for an injection. This might be for a vitamin booster should the animal be suffering a deficiency and is looking particularly out of condition. In less serious cases the vitamins may be given orally or added to its food. At some time in its life your dog may require a course of antibiotics to ward off or eliminate a particular infection. It is usually best if the dog is restrained by an assistant to prevent the animal from biting or struggling while the veterinarian gives the injection.

Right: Examining a Standard Poodle's teeth for signs of decay. Unfortunately, many dog's teeth today become victim to a diet of nothing but canned food, which is well-balanced nutritionally but is not so good for the health of your dog's gums and teeth. In the wild, the teeth are used for killing prey and then eating it raw. Chewing the bones acts as a cleaner and removes any buildup of harmful plaque on the teeth. A bag of bones from the butcher or a handful of dried biscuits given separately or mixed with canned food will help to clean your dog's teeth and keep them healthy.

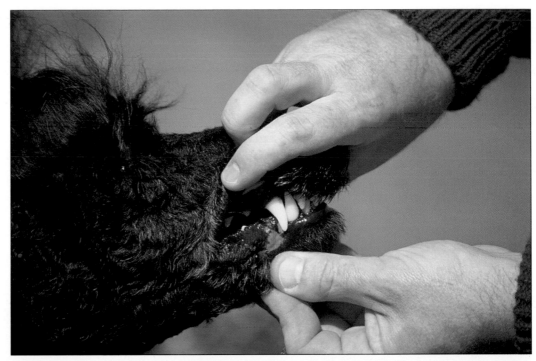

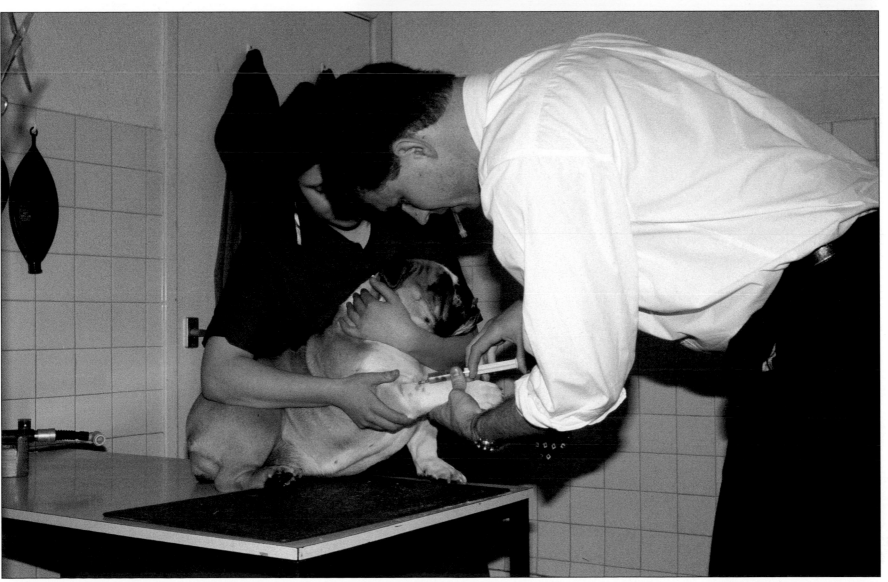

Below: It is acceptable for your dog to sit in the front of the vehicle while it is stationary or parked up for some time. A dog may even act as a useful deterrent to car thieves – but always remember to leave a window slightly open for ventilation (you can buy a gadget to do this safely) – and provide something for the dog to drink during hot weather. A great many dogs die cooped up in hot, airless vehicles every year. But allowing them to go loose should not be encouraged at any time while the car is in motion. Should you ever need to brake suddenly for some reason, your dog could easily be ejected through the windshield, causing severe and even fatal injuries. Also, if the vehicle swerves to avoid a hazard, the dog might tumble between the driver and the steering wheel or the foot pedals, causing the car to go out of control. Some people tether their dogs in the car to prevent this happening or even fit them with special seat belts. To minimize the chances of any mishaps, always put your dogs in the back of the car, preferably with a safety restraint grille between them and the rest of the car. Knowing that your dog is safely restrained in the vehicle also eliminates the chance that it will dangerously distract your driving by becoming unruly or jumping about.

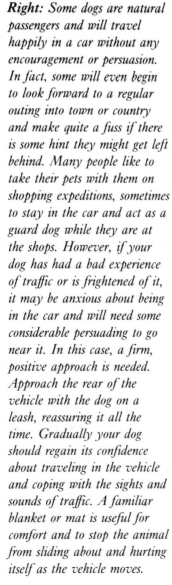

Left: *A small temporary kennel made from lightweight materials is easy to put into the back of a vehicle for convenient transportation. This is a good idea should your dog be nervous of traveling. Most professional kennels use this method for taking their dogs from one place to another because it not only prevents the dog from knocking itself, but also avoids any possibility of the animal biting or causing trouble by becoming uncontrollable in a bid to get away during the journey. This might be especially important if the animal is diseased.*

Right: *Some dogs are natural passengers and will travel happily in a car without any encouragement or persuasion. In fact, some will even begin to look forward to a regular outing into town or country and make quite a fuss if there is some hint they might get left behind. Many people like to take their pets with them on shopping expeditions, sometimes to stay in the car and act as a guard dog while they are at the shops. However, if your dog has had a bad experience of traffic or is frightened of it, it may be anxious about being in the car and will need some considerable persuading to go near it. In this case, a firm, positive approach is needed. Approach the rear of the vehicle with the dog on a leash, reassuring it all the time. Gradually your dog should regain its confidence about traveling in the vehicle and coping with the sights and sounds of traffic. A familiar blanket or mat is useful for comfort and to stop the animal from sliding about and hurting itself as the vehicle moves.*

Below: Reputed to be one of the oldest British breeds, the Otterhound is also one of the easiest dogs to keep fit and healthy, providing you give it the opportunity to take plenty of exercise. It also requires regular grooming because the coat is rough and very dense so easily becomes greasy from the natural oils secreted by the skin. Lots of stamina and an oily coat make this a perfect outdoor dog that would ideally suit the kind of family that enjoys walking and the outdoor life. This breed is resistant to the cold and loves the water – another advantage of an oily coat. Webbed toes make it an excellent swimmer. This is one of the reasons why it used to be so popular in the past for hunting otters, as its name suggests. The dog makes a loyal and devoted family pet, even to the point of standing its ground to protect family members should it consider them to be threatened.

Right: Surprisingly, the Bassett Hound also requires plenty of exercise and a generous diet to stay healthy. They should feed from a narrow bowl to prevent those floppy ears from trailing in the food. To prevent infection, clean the ears regularly with a ball of moist absorbent cotton.

Above: The distinctive and beautiful Dalmatian increased in popularity after the success of the film 'One Hundred and One Dalmatians'. Oddly enough, the dark spots do not appear on the newly born pups until they are about one year old and fully developed. Dalmatians have a good appetite for food and need grooming more or less every day to stay in tiptop condition. Exercise is important to keep that lean muscular body in trim, so it is important for the dog to be allowed to run freely. Dalmatians make very affectionate family pets and are particularly good with children. These are attractive dogs - the visual impact of a bitch and her mature spotted pups can be quite stunning.

Above right: Two Brittany Spaniel pups enjoying an outdoor romp. They are going to need a good deal of training and plenty of exercise to keep them contented and out of mischief. This is a breed that loves the outdoor life and they are very keen hunters. The Brittany Spaniel's compact size helps it to squeeze through the thickest of bushes. Its coat will need to be washed and groomed at least once or twice a week to keep it clean and to maintain good general health.

Right: The Norfolk Terrier makes an ideal pet for both the indoor and outdoor type of person, providing the dog has a regular run in a park or nearby field. The rough wiry coat needs to be groomed every day to keep it in condition.

Dogs at work

Every day, all over the world, dogs prove skilled and invaluable helpmates in the workplace, whether assisting a sophisticated drug or explosives squad or penning sheep on some remote hillside. The working dog is certainly not a modern concept; after all, once the dog had been semi-domesticated, its first role was to help man hunt for food and to act as a guard. In the twentieth century, that usefulness has been extended to maximize the dog's natural talents: loyalty, intelligence, a keen sense of smell and, when necessary, ferocity and strength. Some breeds have proved to be specially suited to a particular task; for example, the sled dogs' hardiness helps them survive the harshest weather conditions and their strong pack instinct means they work well as a team. The Bloodhound, with its extraordinary sense of smell, is still used by the police as a tracker. Many other breeds have been developed to suit a particular purpose and to cope with local conditions. Every country has its favorite stock dog, all as varied as the lives they lead. The hardy Australian Cattle Dog was specially bred to drive semi-wild cattle long distances. Its short, speckled coat provides a good camouflage and resists bad weather with hardly any grooming. How different it is in appearance from the shaggy, good-natured and sometimes obstinate Puli, which is nimble for its size and looks just like a big rug. For centuries, the Puli has worked as a sheepdog on the Hungarian plains. Alternatively, compare the woolly Old English Sheepdog with the short-legged Welsh Corgi - once a cattle dog - and the sharp-faced Shetland Sheepdog from Scotland. With their strong territorial instincts and fighting potential, dogs make good guards too. The heavily built, aggressive Mastiff has always been a favorite for this job, and the savage, but fiercely protective Rottweiler, muscular Dobermann and extremely intelligent German Shepherd Dog are equally popular these days for security work. Many of the spitz type dogs are still in service as sled dogs. We tend to call them all huskies, but this name applies to only one of the breeds specially adapted to sub-zero conditions and the rigors of pulling a heavy load at speed on the minimum of rations. There are many other dogs with the necessary thick double coat and powerful physique: the Samoyed from Siberia, for example, or the Eskimo Dog, a native of the Canadian Arctic. Because most of these dogs live in some of the most inhospitable parts of the world, they have remained extremely true to breed. Completely different skills are called for when dogs are required to help in less wild walks of life. The Frenchman in the Perigord Region is justifiably proud of his truffle-hunting dog; its keen sense of smell could earn him thousands of francs. And, of course, the blind person's guide dog must be intelligent, even-natured and obedient.

Left: With a reputation as the best of all tracker dogs, the Bloodhound has the keenest sense of smell of any domestic animal and a solemn expression as befits a police assistant.

Right: A dog specially trained to scent drugs or explosives is invaluable at a busy terminus where thousands of people and their baggage are constantly on the move.

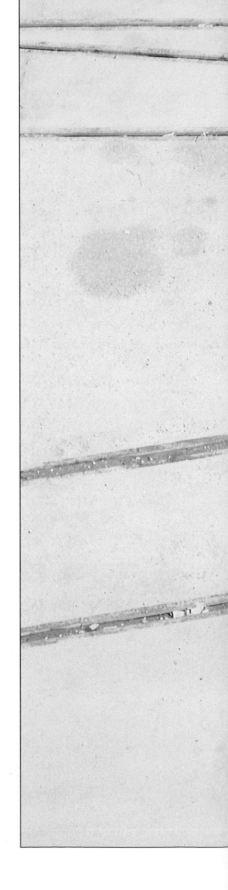

Right: It takes a special kind of dog to be able to cope with the rigorous training demanded of police dogs, and many do not make the grade through lack of courage or ferocity. Total obedience is vitally important, of course, and in most cases a dog is deliberately trained to respond only to the commands of its particular trainer. The German Shepherd dog is a prime example. Intelligent and obedient, it is easily trained for any role from guard to tracker or lifesaver. Training must begin at ten weeks old.

Right: Gotcha! A crook is apprehended as he makes his getaway. Most police forces include a dog handling unit and many have been using dogs for years to assist in combating crime. Normally the dog is taught to catch hold of the arm holding the weapon, but in this case it has been made to latch onto the other. Protective pads are worn in training to make sure the dog's teeth do not cause any damage. Other areas, such as the legs, can also be padded to train the dogs to bite the lower part of the body and immobilize the 'intruder'.

Below: Not all working dogs are pedigree breeds; some are a mixture of several suitable types. This Old English Sheepdog/Border Collie cross has all the makings of a first-class working stock dog. The Border Collie element gives it the sense to go out and round up the waiting stock slowly and patiently, and also provides the speed required to outmaneuver and overtake the herd should it make a dash for freedom. The Old English Sheepdog genes contribute the size and toughness required for moving and turning sheep or cattle. Sometimes a cow makes a defiant stand and the dog needs the courage to stand up to her, snapping and snarling until it has forced her to join the rest of the herd. Stock dogs must be able to work in all weathers, from the blazing heat of summer to the bleakest and harshest of winters. These are usually extremely loyal dogs and only take orders from one master, especially if the relationship is long established. For all their spirit and roughness with larger animals, they can be remarkably gentle with newborn stock. Their ability to adapt to each new situation is one of their assets.

Right: The magnificent Briard has the appearance of a huge cuddly toy and for many years was considered to be one of the best sheepdogs. At one time, shepherds would use several of these dogs to watch over their flocks and could rely on them to keep hundreds of grazing sheep together, with hardly a word of command or encouragement. Today, the Briard's popularity on the farm has declined, as smaller dogs have been adapted for the task. However, the police and security firms quite often use the breed, as it makes an excellent tracker and good guard dog. The Briard was used during the First World War by French soldiers at the front line to carry ammunition and first-aid equipment. The dog was also found to play a useful role in locating injured men.

Left: The Boxer makes an ideal family pet, but can also prove an effective guard dog should it be put to the test. It was originally bred as a hunting dog and its ancestors would courageously go after wild boar and bears. Later it was valued for cattle herding and driving, and is still a brave and energetic animal, although these days the Boxer is more likely to spend its days snoozing and playing the part of family pet and guardian. It does enjoy plenty of exercise, so be prepared to take it out for long, frequent walks and allow it to run loose. Before letting it off the leash, make sure there is no livestock about that the dog may be tempted to chase. And keep an eye open for other dogs, too; they sometimes view the stocky Boxer as a potential threat.

Left: The rugged Eskimo dog is renowned for its hardiness and ability to work well in freezing conditions. This is the dog that has helped many explorers to cross the Canadian Arctic, which is its native home. The Eskimo people rely on these beautiful and devoted dogs throughout the year, but especially in the winter months when harsh conditions make life very difficult. These are powerful dogs and when several of them are harnessed together, they are capable of pulling a sled weighing several hundreds of pounds across the snow and ice. The dog is also used for hunting and can locate the breathing holes made by seals in the thick ice. They have been known to stand their ground when faced with a polar bear, so clearly they do not lack in courage.

Right: The Bull Mastiff was specially developed as a guard dog and was once popular with gamekeepers, who would take the dog with them on their regular rounds at night as they kept a watch for poachers. The dog was trained to attack quickly but quietly and this probably explains how it came to be known – and once feared – as the 'Gamekeeper's Nightdog'. Today, this intelligent animal is often used by the police. The dog was originally bred by crossing the British Bulldog with the Mastiff – both potentially aggressive breeds. In the wrong hands, this agile and powerful breed can be rather vicious and certainly requires firm handling and control from an early age. Groom the coat every day to keep it in top condition and give the dog a regular bath if it is usually exercised in the countryside.

Left: We all think of the Saint Bernard as a great shaggy bearlike dog, with the familiar brandy cask around its neck. This almost legendary mountain rescue dog is still used in the alpine regions where it began its working career, taking its name from the St. Bernard Hospice in the Swiss Alps, and it must have saved the lives of thousands of walkers and climbers over the years. The huge nose and muzzle endow it with a remarkable sense of smell and the dog seems to have a kind of sixth sense that enables it to foresee sudden storms and avalanches. These days, other breeds are also used for rescue work alongside the Saint Bernard, but it will surely be the dog most closely associated with safety on the mountains.

Left: A proud Rottweiler. Bad publicity concerning the dog's aggressiveness has made this breed something of an outlaw in recent years, but most have an easygoing and calm temperament. It is likely that mishandling and poor training of such spirited and potentially fierce breeds has led to them becoming unnecessarily aggressive towards humans and other animals. This behavior may also be an outlet for boredom and frustration. In Austria, intelligent and eager-to-learn Rottweilers are frequently used to accompany the police in their line of duty. Correctly trained, a Rottweiler makes a good, hardworking guard dog and it is often to be found patrolling factories and business establishments. Its name and reputation were earned hundreds of years ago, when the profitable cattle-rearing villagers of Rottweil used these intelligent, reliable dogs as guards to protect them from bandits as they traveled to market. They fastened purses of money to the dogs' collars.

Right: This Australian Cattle Dog, sometimes also called the Queensland Heeler, is an extremely tough and hard-working stockman's dog, capable of tolerating the harsh conditions of Australia's treacherous outback. It was bred for the specific purpose of herding and protecting wild cattle over many long and dusty miles. It uses its powerful jaw to good effect to nip at the legs of any strays that dare stand up to it. Specially bred for the rough and tumble of this hard outdoor life, the Australian Cattle Dog needs very little care, other than an occasional good brushing. The breed is the successful result of crossing Collies with Dingoes.

75

Above: There are three breed variations of Schnauzer. The Standard breed shown here is the oldest. At one time, they accompanied stagecoaches over long distances, keeping pace with the teams of horses. It was also used to keep the mice and rat population down in the towns and earned its reputation because it was easy to train and work with. You will often see the Standard Schnauzer depicted in old paintings. The Giant Schnauzer was more favored in the past as a cattle dog, guarding the stock against rustlers and wild animals.

They were only really phased out with the arrival of the steam age and trains, which meant that it was more convenient to transport cattle in freight cars instead of walking them many miles to different markets. There is also a Miniature Schnauzer, a smaller version of the Standard type. This is the dog preferred in the home, as it is not only a good family pet but also a useful guard dog, being obedient but affectionate towards all members of the family. All types of Schnauzer require plenty of exercise and regular grooming.

Right: Dogs that have been trained to assist the blind can relieve an unsighted person of part of their handicap. The training is lengthy and the dogs must show a particular aptitude for the work from an early age. Only when the instructors are satisfied that the animal is fully competent will it be allotted to its new owner. The blind person also receives instruction on how to handle and control their new chaperone. After the two have become acquainted and are used to one another, all the necessary commands are well rehearsed before they venture out together. Funds for the training of these dogs are often raised on a voluntary basis.

Left: The Dobermann Pinscher is named after the founder of the breed, a tax collecter named Louis Dobermann, who achieved the dog he was seeking in 1899 after successfully crossing several other types. It is a first-class guard dog and frequently used as such by security firms. Dobermanns are often seen patrolling perimeter fences; they will stand firm against any intruder and when confronted can be quite ferocious when trained to be so. The dog's natural instinct to stand its ground can be identified from an early age and this characteristic also makes it a popular breed for police work.

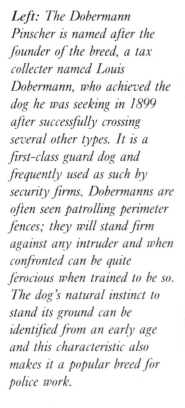

Dogs in sport

The fiercest dogs have been pitched against each other for sport at least since Roman times, and while such barbaric practices are largely outlawed these days, some of the old fighting breeds, such as the Bulldog and Bull Terrier, survive to this day, albeit with much of their aggression bred out of them. Today, we prefer to match our dogs on the racecourse. In the UK greyhounds are kept almost exclusively for their superb turn of speed, although a few are kept as pets. The Greyhound has been prized for thousands of years as a fleet-footed hunter and the breed remains relatively pure. Its lean profile and powerful muscles enable this dog to reach speeds of up to 44mph (70kph), but its diet and exercise must be carefully monitored to keep it in champion condition. In some parts of the world dogs are still used to hunt for food, but as man's dependence on the wild diminishes and many of the big game animals are hunted out of existence, the specially bred dogs are also disappearing or becoming rarer. What would have become of the efficient wolf hunters, such as the Irish Wolfhound or Bleu de Gascoigne, if it were not for keen breeders and people prepared to keep them as pets? Hunting is still a popular sport, whether it be big-game hunting in South Africa with a pack of Rhodesian Ridgebacks to rout out the lions or tracking deer and wild boar in Japan, with the help of an Akita. This quiet and attractive dog had the courage to hunt black bears when they were still widespread. Other dogs have been bred over the centuries to tackle smaller game, as well as local predators and vermin. The hunt for fox, hare and stag, is traditionally accompanied by a pack of Hounds, Harriers or Beagles, and their stamina and enthusiasm, regardless of the weather, is legendary. Terriers are masters at tirelessly hunting rats, rabbits and other small vermin, which they do with relish and enjoyment. The larger terriers are excellent fox hunters, too. But top of the class for skill and obedience must be the world's gundogs; pointers, setters and retrievers are expertly trained in the hunting of small game and game birds on land and water. Each breed has a particular talent from which it may have taken its name: pointers locate the quarry and then freeze in position, pointing at the spot with the muzzle or paw until ordered to flush it out. A setter is similarly skilled, crouching motionlessly once it has scented a bird. Retrievers have a powerful jaw for carrying waterlogged or heavy game, but a soft mouth so that they do not damage prey.

Left: The well-trained gundog, such as this Small Munsterlander, must have stamina and initiative to flush out and retrieve wild game from lake or thicket in the course of a long day. Yet the dog must also be totally obedient, returning its quarry completely unmarked and unmolested.

Below: Huskies and other spitz-type snow dogs are winning new respect for their strength, endurance and superb team spirit in the world of sport. The Siberian Husky has been the undisputed sled-racing champion since a team of these dogs entered and won the All-Alaska Sweepstake Race at the beginning of the twentieth century. Polar explorers valued their calm temperament and stamina in harsh conditions.

Right: The Pointer is a very good hunting dog; in fact, it has earned a reputation among many shooting sportsmen as being one of the best. Its powerful nose helps it to track down and locate game in the thickest of bushes. Then, when it has found where the quarry is hiding out, it will freeze on the spot and take up a stance with all the beauty and graceful stillness of a ballet dancer. Its nose will point towards the bush or cover where the game is hiding and the dog will remain in this position until its master commands it to go in and flush it out. Sometimes the Pointer raises one leg to point in the same direction as its nose and the dog has been known to stand in this position for hours. Most Pointers are excellent all-round gundogs.

Right: Game fairs and dog shows throughout the world sometimes have an area set aside where sporting men and women can compete with their dogs, rather in the manner of sheepdog trials. Game is placed within the confines of a predetermined course and the owners have to communicate with their dogs from a distance by using a whistle and verbal or hand signals. There is usually a target time to beat and the course can be very demanding; the dogs may even have to cross a lake or river and negotiate a wood or rough slope on the other side. Having successfully located the game, the dog must then return it to base as quickly as possible. In a real hunting situation, 'picker-uppers' are sometimes paid to bring their dogs along to retrieve any birds that land in inaccessible places.

Above right: Beagle Hounds eagerly waiting for the day's sport to begin. Every pack has a leader, even when the dogs are a domesticated breed, and he or she leads the other dogs on the field until they go their separate ways. It is possible to identify the leader even before the hunt begins, as shown here. It is usually the older, stronger dog that keeps the rest of the pack in order.

Right: This Weimaraner is successfully retrieving game from the water. Originally used for hunting big game in its native Germany, this dog was later developed for hunting and retrieving smaller game birds. Its intelligence and strong muscular body have made it an ideal subject for training as a powerful swimmer, and the Weimeraner is a first-classs water dog.

Below: The Pharaoh Hound is a good choice for the all-round sportsman, being an excellent retriever and hardy hunting dog. It uses its remarkable sense of smell and keen eyesight, unlike most of the hound family, which hunt on scent alone. Its body length and sleek shape, combined with strong muscular legs, give it the speed and flexibility to match most wild animals over rough ground, and it requires a lot of exercise. It is believed to be related to the ancient Greyhound and certainly resembles the elegant but agile-looking dogs associated with Ancient Egypt, hence its name.

Right: The beautiful Saluki usually hunts with a falcon that flies high in the air to spot the quarry. Then it swoops down and circles until the prey can be flushed out for the speedy Saluki to chase.

Above: The Rhodesian Ridgeback is not, as its name suggests, from the country now called Zimbabwe, but it did originate in South Africa and packs of dogs are still used for hunting there. The Ridgeback is renowned for the great courage it displays when hunting lions and big game, which the pack pursues relentlessly. The dogs are taken to the area where the quarry is likely to be found and are then released in order to drive the frightened prey towards the waiting guns. It is said that should one of these dogs confront a lion, it will bravely stand its ground and try to keep the beast there until the hunters catch up. The dog gets its name from the crest of hair that grows along its back in the opposite direction to the rest of the coat. Despite its reputation as a daring and savage hunter, the Rhodesian Ridgeback can be just as happy leading a rather less exciting life as a large but active family pet. Providing it is allowed access to plenty of space for exercise and is given a firm hand, it can make a good-natured companion.

Left: The Irish Setter, or Red Setter, is very robust and energetic, not suited to a quiet urban life, but perfect in an outdoor country habitat where it has access to plenty of open space to burn off all that energy. Its soft muzzle and love of the water make it an ideal all-round companion for the shooting sportsman, as it expertly flushes out and carefully retrieves game birds.

Below: The Japanese Akita is a beautiful and skilled hunter of wild boar, deer and even bear. Sadly, it was also popular as a public fighting dog for many years, which almost led to its extinction. Today, the Akita's numbers are on the increase again and this athletic, affectionate animal is a popular pet, police and guard dog, as well as a hunter.

Left: At the end of a long and exciting day's shoot, both dog and owner will feel tired but satisfied. Here, a Small Munsterlander sits quietly with the partridge it has retrieved. Sporting dogs need plenty of regular exercise all year round.

Below: Another superb hunting dog, the English Setter, is both loyal and good-natured, only becoming restless if it does not have enough outdoor exercise. Its thick coat is ideal for withstanding winter weather and muddy waters.

Right: *The Jack Russell may not be fully recognized as an official breed, but it is hugely popular, especially in the UK, where this lively little terrier is an enthusiastic hunter of small rodents and rabbits. It works well in conjunction with a ferret and makes an amusing if boisterous pet in a family home or on the farm, where it will work well for its keep.*

Below: *The Lurcher is another unrecognized breed, a rangy-looking cross between a terrier and a greyhound. However, it is highly valued for its after-dark hunting skills. True to its reputation as a poacher's dog, the lean Lurcher appears to slink like a shadow and will sidle alongside the beam of a torch or lamp to seize an unsuspecting rabbit.*

Right: The Greyhound's legendary speed makes it well suited to the role of hunting dog. Centuries before it became popular for racing, it was highly valued for its ability to outpace stag, fox and hare. It was in an attempt to find a more humane sport as an alternative to hare coursing, that track racing was introduced in the late 19th century. The Greyhound needs plenty of vitamins and minerals to stay in peak condition and careful feeding or it will lose its sleek shape. It naturally requires plenty of exercise and should be allowed to run freely a couple of times a week. Although still used for hunting, and popularly kept as a quiet but intelligent pet, the Greyhound is mostly bred for racing and shows.

Dogs on a grand scale

Strangely enough, large dogs are impressive but rarely intimidating, despite their great bulk and size. Unlike smaller dogs, they are not inclined to be aggressive with strangers, unless specifically trained as a guard dog. Larger dogs tend to be the gentler breeds, good-natured and affectionate. They make excellent family pets for people with the space and resources to keep them, for they are very good with children. Most were originally bred as guard dogs, hunters and sheepdogs. They are strong enough to withstand hard outdoor living conditions, intelligent enough to understand specific commands and remain totally obedient. A few big dogs still earn their living in the traditional way. For example, in its native Turkey, the white-coated Kuvasz was originally used as a guard dog by both the shepherd and the rich landowner to defend their property. These days it is a popular guard dog for police and military duties. In the snowy regions of Hungary, the police use another large sheepdog, the shaggy Komondor, as a tracker dog. It is ideally adapted to the harsh climate and conditions and capable of traveling long distances in a day. The big, friendly-looking Saint Bernard is renowned in the Alps for its uncanny skill in locating climbers and walkers in trouble. Another big rescue dog is the Newfoundland, a massive animal with a thick, slightly oily coat, as powerful in water as it is on land. Because it is easily trained and loves water, it has been used extensively not only to rescue drowning people, but also to drag to shore any boats that are in trouble. This versatile dog is also a good hunter and guard dog. Usually it is the mountain breeds that are massively built, muscular and with good thick coats. The Swiss Mountain dogs are a typical example, commonly used to herd stock and generally act as guard dogs, but these beautiful animals have a good nature and great strength to tackle a wide variety of jobs around the farm. The handsome Leonberger is a possible Saint Bernard/Newfoundland crossbreed. Its coat is usually a wonderful golden color, with a

big, shaggy mane like a huge friendly lion. Like many big dogs, the intelligent Leonberger is very protective towards children, but when trained as a family guard dog it can be fierce towards strangers. Some big dogs are less cuddly. The Great Dane, or German Mastiff, is tall, with a muscular, shorthaired body that makes it a popular show dog. Despite its proud and powerful stance, this dog is affectionate and patient with children. The largest dog of all is the Irish Wolfhound, weighing about 110lb(50kg). It is immensely tall and muscular but graceful, and covered in coarse wiry hair worn a little long over the eyes and under the jaw, giving the dog a slightly rakish air. Despite its rather bloodthirsty past and rough appearance, the Wolfhound is quiet and friendly, providing it is given plenty of outdoor exercise.

Left: Bernese Mountain dogs were bred as hardworking farm dogs but make excellent family companions, being loyal, intelligent and affectionate. They do not react well to a change of owner and may become difficult as a result.

Right: The beautiful Afghan Hound is wonderfully graceful for a large dog. Despite its haughty good looks, it is devoted and affectionate. Desert peoples have long prized its speed and stamina over difficult terrain, making it an invaluable hunting companion.

Below: Once a sheepdog, today the Briard is a popular guide dog for the blind and valued as a good mountain rescue and police dog.

Above: The Irish Wolfhound, as it name suggests, was once used for hunting wolves, its size and strength being more than a match even for the wolf. The practice of hunting wolves was phased out during the eighteenth century when the number of wolves had diminished and the animal had become virtually extinct in Europe. From this time onwards, the Wolfhound became more domesticated. As a rather outsize pet – the Irish Wolfhound is one of the largest dogs in the world – its enthusiasm for the hunt has been converted into a lively playfulness and an easygoing, friendly nature. Naturally, this giant of a dog – it can measure up to 38in(98cm) tall at the highest point of the back – still requires a great deal of exercise and, given the opportunity, will tear across an open space with obvious glee. The hardy Wolfhound is not one of the aristocrats of the dog world. Its coat is rather rough and hairy – no doubt a useful feature for an animal designed to cope with cold climates and wet weather conditions. It needs regular brushing with a metal comb or stiff-bristled brush to prevent it from taking on a rather disreputable appearance. The Wolfhound's diet should consist of a high proportion of meat and calcium in order to maintain strong healthy bones.

Right: The Old English Sheepdog is a popular breed among many breeders of large dogs. It was originally bred and developed in the UK, to the west of the country, by farmers and shepherds who were looking for a good, tough working dog. Several different working breeds were used to make up this sheepdog, both native breeds and others imported from various European countries. Today, it is still used for work, as well as being kept as a pet. In the shearing season it is often shorn along with the sheep to keep it clean and cool throughout the summer. The hair grows back quickly, so the dog is still assured of a thick coat for the next cold winter.

Left: The large Newfoundland is justly famous worldwide as a courageous yet placid big breed. Its strength and intelligence and strong swimming ability make it the ideal all-round rescue dog.

Above: The large, impressive Neapolitan Mastiff has earned a considerable reputation as one of the most fearsome modern guard dogs. The Italian armed forces and police use it for extra support during troubles, and also as a routine worker and companion. Although it makes a loyal pet, it has to be said that unless this dog is properly trained in the early stages of its life and firmly handled thereafter, it can become a very dangerous and fierce dog indeed, capable of severing a limb with its powerful jaws. This after all was what it was used and bred for in ancient times.

Right: The handsome Borzoi is sometimes called the Russian Wolfhound, as this member of the Greyhound family was used in Imperial Russia in the 17th century for wolf hunting. The Grand Duke Nicholas had an impressive kennel of about 150 of these magnificent dogs. The sport presented few problems in terms of actually catching a wolf, as the country was literally overrun by them until they died out at the beginning of the 19th century A quiet and faithful breed, the Borzoi eventually became popular as a rather impressive pet for those with homes large enough to keep them.

Left: *The Great Dane is well known throughout the canine world and is especially popular in North America, where the breed is more docile. When properly trained, it makes an excellent guard dog, capable of warding off anyone that dares to confront it. Good training in the first stages of its life is absolutely essential, as early neglect will inevitably lead to problems later on. When the dogs are small, their master can generally dominate them, but problems caused by lack of training increase when dealing with a huge, fully grown adult Great Dane.*

Right: *A Giant Schnauzer and pup. As well as this bigger type, there are also two smaller ones, namely the Standard breed, which is probably the original breed from which the Giant developed, and also the Miniature. All three are almost identical in looks, but differ quite considerably in size. This particular Giant breed needs plenty of exercise in order to maintain its fitness and help to establish a pattern of settled behavior. A firm hand is required to control the Schnauzer when it is being trained for life in a domestic situation, as it can be very stubborn and likes to have its own way. All three dogs in the Schnauzer family need to be groomed on a daily basis to keep them looking in peak condition. They have a dense wiry outer coat and a thick underfur, usually black or salt-and-pepper speckled.*

Left: Like many large dogs, the Belgian Tervueren is a traditional herding breed, one of three recognized types of Belgian Shepherd dog. The breed almost died out after the First World War and it was the long-coated Groenendael that was favored by breeders for revival. Nevertheless, the Tervueren has survived, an intelligent and hardy dog that responds well to firm but kind handling. It has an attractive red, fawn or gray coat marked with black. Given plenty of outdoor exercise, it will settle to life in an apartment.

Above: Good-natured and hardworking, the Airedale is the largest breed in the terrier family. Unlike most of the other terrier types, it is not able to pursue rabbits down their burrows, but can prove an excellent ratter. A powerful muscular jaw and strong teeth have made it a formidable hunter and it is an extremely good swimmer. It has excellent sight and hearing, a good sense of smell, great strength and tackles any task with tireless enthusiasm, but such energy needs a firm, affectionate hand from an early age.

Right: The Clumber Spaniel is not tall, but it is a very solid-looking dog considering its playful nature and early reputation as a hardworking packhound. The body is long and low with strong muscular shoulders. The massive head with its large, drooping ears is solid, with a heavy muzzle. The long, silky coat needs regular grooming, especially if the dog lives indoors, paying special attention to the ears. The Clumber's heavy physique makes it very unlike any other breed of spaniel, yet it is still a good sporting dog.

Left: The Pyrenean Mountain Dog is distinctive, not just for its size, but also for its beautiful thick white coat. Terrifically strong and as solid-looking as a bear, the Mountain Dog was once employed in guarding stock in the Pyrenees. Later it became a popular guard dog in France and while it is most definitely not suitable as a house dog, it does make an affectionate and obedient family pet.

Right: With its handsome physique and beautiful red color, the Irish, or Red, Setter is highly prized as a show dog, as well as a hunting dog. Nevertheless, it is a first-class sportsman's dog, prized all over the world for its speed and stamina and its talents as a pointer and excellent water retriever. Firm handling and plenty of exercise will temper its rather lively temperament. It is affectionate and loyal.

Right: A Leonberger family, with a pup shown left, bitch at center and dog on the right. The breed is possibly a shaggy cross between a Newfoundland and a Saint Bernard. Not surprisingly, therefore, these are big dogs - and very lovable. Like most mountain dogs, they are real gentle giants: affectionate and loyal, yet strong and brave enough to make top-class guard dogs. Although they can be fierce when challenged, and are particularly protective towards children, they do not bark much, which makes them an excellent family house guard, providing you can give them plenty of exercise every day. A thick woolly golden coat and appealing brown eyes only add to their endearing charm.

The charm of small dogs

Many of the smaller dogs such as terriers are not as delicate as they might at first appear. Originally bred as hunting animals, often intended to work in groups or packs, they tend to be tough, rough and joyful. However, dogs specially bred for their diminutive size, such as the toy and miniature breeds, are frequently a different matter. The fashion for small breeds probably originated in Ancient China or Mexico and eventually became popular throughout the world, tiny dogs being developed through selective breeding. This has lead to congenital problems, such as abnormally short legs and bulging eyes, as well as dislocation of certain bones. While small dogs look very cute and can be affectionate towards their owners, they have rather short tempers as a rule and will be aggressive or snappy with strangers. This does make them useful small guard dogs. They are not always ideally suited as family pets - as we have seen, the docile big breeds are surprisingly good with children - but the more sedate small breeds are perfectly cast as the pampered companions of apartment dwellers. Small dogs were once the prize of royalty and the rich. Queens, princesses and the finest ladies throughout the centuries, from Ancient China and Japan to the courts of Europe, have had their favorite breeds, which they would pet on their lap, carry around in their sleeves or hang round their neck in a basket - almost like an ornament. Because the dog was regarded as a fashion accessory, it is not surprising that most of the miniature or toy lapdog breeds are the prettiest. Many look little more than

bundles of fluff, their hair sometimes tied back with a ribbon and always beautifully groomed. A small dog may not be as costly to feed and needs less exercise - although a few types need a surprising amount - but they can be very time-consuming, especially the longhaired breeds. The ornamental Lhasa Apso needs daily brushing and combing to keep its long, thick hair looking good. The Shih Tzu is another delightful head-to-toe furball with a coat that must be kept in tiptop condition. These long-coated dogs naturally have a rather oriental appearance - and indeed, many originated in China or Tibet. However, the elegant Papillon is a product of the Renaissance courts of Italy. You can see its spaniel antecedents in the shape of the body, but the dog is wholly aristocratic, with its big feathery ears and lively nature. There are miniaturized and toy versions of some popular dog breeds, such as the Poodle, for people who do not have the space for a bigger dog. There is also a range of smooth-haired, wire-coated or long-haired Miniature Dachshunds. The tiny Pinscher is an alert and intelligent guard dog despite its size. The smallest dog in the world is the Chihuahua, which can be smooth- or long-coated. Despite weighing only 2.2lb(1kg), this little dog needs plenty of exercise.

Above: The Smooth-haired Fox Terrier has been popular since the 1860s, when it gained a reputation as a good ratter. It has always been a favorite pet as well as a reliable hunting dog.

Left: The Yorkshire Terrier needs special grooming before a show. Its hair must be trimmed, washed and dried to avoid any knots or curls. A ribbon is often used to keep the hair from the eyes.

Right: It is the Papillon's ears that give it such a decorative air of elegance and charm. Large and fringed like the wings of an exotic butterfly, there are two variations: in the Phalene, or moth, variety the ears droop down towards the face, whereas in the Papillon, or butterfly, they are held erect. The Papillon also has a delightful nature, which has made it a favorite for centuries, being gentle and affectionate, yet playful, too.

Below: The tiny Pekingese is certainly exotic: its hair is thick and luxurious with feathering about the ears, legs and tail. The wide face, with its dark flat-nosed muzzle, is dominated by large shining eyes. Exclusively the pampered pet of the Chinese royalty for centuries, the Pekingese still enjoys a life of unashamed luxury and would rather sit and be spoiled and petted than take any form of exercise.

Right: At one time the Poodle was not the show animal or pampered pet we are familiar with today, but a popular gundog and water retriever. It is mainly the trim that makes it look so comical; this was originally designed to help the dog swim more easily. The miniature apricot and black poodles shown here have been given a Country clip. There is even a 'dreadlocks' Poodle called the Corded.

Above: *The Longhaired Dachshund is one of six variations of the breed: three are standard - the Longhaired, Smooth-haired and the Wire-haired. Then there are the miniature versions of each of these three types. The name Dachshund means 'badger dog' in German and it was once used for badger hunting. The Dachshund's distinctive long body and short legs enabled it to slither down the smallest lairs and either flush out the badgers or physically drag them to the surface. These merry little dogs can give their owners much pleasure, but they can have a stubborn streak.*

Right: *The rugged Cairn Terrier, like many other small breeds of dog, was originally bred for a specific hunting purpose, namely to rid the many Ancient Roman burial grounds throughout the Scottish Highlands of rodents, foxes and weasels. The dog's ability to dig up gardens - irrespective of what is planted there - in its enthusiasm to root out rodents has given the Cairn a bad name among keen gardeners. Gradually it becomes very devoted to its owners, with a tendency towards jealousy, especially when a new member of the family is introduced.*

Far left, left and below: Small dogs will always be popular as friendly household companions and there is certainly a wide variety of cheeky characters to choose from. The lively Jack Russell (below) may not have a pedigree but is quick to learn and full of tricks. The smallest breed of dog of all, the novelty Chihuahua (left) is popular largely because it is so tiny - less than 2.2lb(1kg). Much more rarely seen is the Petit Basset Griffon Vendeen (far left) - a miniature variety of the good-looking but bushy-haired Griffon Vendeen, once a great French hunting dog.

Left: The small but shaggy Chinese 'lion dog', or Shih Tzu, charms everyone with its playful nature, large dark eyes peeping out of long hair and plumed tail. It loves to be spoiled and adapts well to life in an apartment with a doting owner, whom it will repay with unwavering loyalty. Despite its size, this dog needs plenty of exercise and a careful diet if it is not to put on weight. Groom the coat every day and give the dog a bath every five or six weeks to keep it looking at its best. The Shih Tzu's exact origins are unclear. It is believed to be related to the Lhasa Apso and an early type of Pekingese.

Right: This delicate-looking little lapdog with its feathery ears and tail is in fact a robust and lively Tibetan Spaniel. It makes an affectionate pet, but does not warm to strangers. These popular show dogs require daily grooming.

Right: The bright-eyed Pomeranian is the smallest of the spitz breeds and features the distinctive plumed tail that curls over the back. This compact, well-tempered breed has enjoyed periods of being highly fashionable, but in the Middle Ages it was probably a working sled dog. It has often appealed to royalty. Queen Victoria encouraged selective breeding, which has produced today's particularly tiny dogs. One of the drawbacks to inbreeding has been a range of hereditary diseases. Being quick to learn and lively, the Pomeranian has also been a favored breed for the circus, where its deep bark but diminutive size adds to its appeal as a performer.

Right: The French Bulldog is an affectionate and placid animal that happily plays with children yet also makes the ideal loyal companion for an elderly person. It cannot tolerate high temperatures and is susceptible to sunstroke.

Below: The Cavalier King Charles Spaniel, or English Toy Spaniel, is a deliberate attempt to get back to the old breed of Spaniel seen in paintings by Gainsborough and Rembrandt. The breeding program was begun in the 1920s by an American, Roswell Eldridge, and the dog was officially recognized in 1945. The head of the Cavalier has a different shape from the more modern King Charles Spaniel, which has more prominent eyes, the ears set lower and a shorter muzzle with a snub nose. This attempt to restore a more ancient breed has apparently revived some of its old instincts too, as the Cavalier is recognizably a hunting dog as it was in the days of Mary Stuart of England - although King Charles II, who gave his name to the breed, preferred to keep his large collection as pets. There are four coat types and the Cavalier does not vary from these: a Black and Tan; the Ruby, which is a chestnut color; the Blenheim, with red patches on white; and the Prince Charles - white with black markings and tan patches. The dogs should be given a thorough daily grooming, paying special attention to the ears and eyes.

Right: *The ancestors of the Miniature Bull Terrier were once fierce fighters. Today, such dogs are bred for their even temperament and friendly manner, although they have lost none of their alertness. This tiny terrier is no more than 14in(35cm) high, the result of a breeding program begun in the 1920s. It is identical to the Bull Terrier in every way except its size.*

Below: *The Scottie and the Westie make a striking black and white pair. Both are very popular pets, although once vigorous hunters of otter, badger and rodents. The bushy-browed Scottish Terrier is not always even tempered, but the West Highland White Terrier - pure white and far more agreeable in nature is also spirited and amusing.*

Left: Shetland Sheepdogs, or Shelties, as they are sometimes called, are a popular small breed of working dog that make very affectionate and obedient pets to have around. They are probably best suited to a country existence, where they can live life to the full, keeping fit through working and rounding up sheep or taking long exploratory rambles. Today they are very often seen in the show classes, where the dogs' beautiful long coats often catch the judge's eye. This long hair can be a nuisance, as it will literally come out in handfuls when the dog is shedding its coat. You can minimize the problem by grooming the dog regularly, say two or three times a week. This could prove a full-time commitment if you have more than one dog, but your care and attention will be rewarded by loyalty and affection.

Below: Looking little more than a bundle of fluff, the playful Bichon Frise is a perennial favorite. 'Bichon' is French for lapdog and the Bichon Frise has long been the darling of fashionable ladies – at least since the fourteenth century, when it was first introduced to Europe from the Canary Islands. It is equally popular today, particularly in the UK, France, Italy and throughout North America.

The dog is great fun to have around the home, being full of character and lively, but it does need a fair amount of attention. The coat must be groomed every day with a stiff brush and the dog given a bath once a month. The Bichon Frise is prone to eye problems, so it is a good idea to clean the eyes regularly, using a cotton swab dipped in a special solution that you can obtain from your veterinarian.

Dogs with a difference

There are dogs as large as ponies and some as small as a squirrel. Certain breeds look fierce, while others are cuddly or irresistibly soft and appealing - you can find a huge variety of size, shape, color and type among them. But there are a few dogs that stand out from all the rest because they look so strange or simply comical that it is sometimes hard to believe they are dogs at all. Often, these odd-looking animals are the result of an accident of nature that breeders have isolated and turned into a rarity. Other breeds simply have a particularly unusual shape or coat type to suit their native climate or terrain. Because many of these dogs are rare, you do not often see them, which adds to their curiosity value. One example is the San Juan Teotihuacan - a strange dog with a strange name. The Aztec word means 'hairless' and this peculiar animal with its wrinkled skin and ears like leather sails was believed to be a very ancient breed dating back to that remote civilization. The Aztecs also prized another hairless dog that is a little more commonly seen today - the Mexican Hairless. This dainty little dog has soft velvety skin and large ears. Surprisingly, the breed is quite hardy and does not require any special care. You do not need to muffle it up in winter as it enjoys a romp in cold weather. There is another breed closely related to the Mexican Hairless that looks even odder. The hairless Chinese Crested shows off its pastel-shaded, spotted skin, except on the head, paws and tail, where there are tufts of wispy hair. A dog can look equally strange if it has the opposite characteristic - too much hair. Many of the large breeds have a thick woolly coat, but there are two in particular with hair so dense that it is hard to see a dog beneath it at all. Both are Hungarian shepherd dogs from harsh regions, and look very like walking hearth rugs with their thick curly fleece. The Puli has a coat that reaches right to the ground, hiding even its legs, and the pure white Komondor looks very like a sheep itself. It is increasing in popularity in North America as a working dog.

Facial expression reveals a lot, and some dogs just cannot help looking comical. Many breeds are appealing simply because their face is crumpled, like the Pug or the rare Shar Pei, with its skin that looks several sizes to big for it. The Boston Terrier, or Roundhead, has such a squashed-in face that it looks as though it has walked into a wall. Certain dogs have been made to look even stranger by selective breeding or by adapting their features surgically to keep them true to a particular breed type. The Bedlington Terrier, for example, is specially clipped to emphasize its lamblike appearance and strange drooping ears. Docking the tail is common in many dogs, and some have their ears clipped back or even restrained under a cap until they are at the right angle. Not surprisingly, this can lead to discomfort or even medical problems for the dog. Some animals experience breathing difficulties and if the skin becomes so wrinkled around the eyes that the animal cannot see, it has to undergo surgery to correct the problem.

Right: Until very recently, the Chinese Shar Pei (or Shai Pei) was such a curiosity it was virtually extinct - certainly one of the world's rarest breed of dogs. For centuries it was bred as a fighting dog, although today it is a gentle dog unless provoked. Luckily for this funny looking dog with its sagging folds, it caught the imagination of Western dog lovers and there has been a deliberate breeding campaign to save it. Intelligent and easily trained, the Shar Pei justifies its popularity as a pet - it is a faithful and clean house dog that requires little grooming.

Left: You do not often see the Griffon Bruxellois outside its native Belgium - not because its whiskery face and disgruntled expression do not appeal to potential owners, but because of the difficulties in breeding it.

Left: Extremes of climate can create dogs specially adapted to withstand difficult conditions. Many of the mountain working dogs have huge thick pelts and look more like woolly bears. One example is this Italian sheepdog, known as the Bergamasco, or Bergamaschi Herder, rarely seen outside the mountains of Northern Italy, but here exhibited to championship standard. This hardy breed is descended from the herding dogs of Roman times and has probably changed little over many centuries, virtually isolated in its mountain home.

Below: These days, the curly Portuguese Water Dog from the Algarve is rarely required to retrieve anything that might roll overboard, to guard a boat or act as messenger between ship and shore or ship to ship. Indeed, these dogs are rarely seen outside the showring. Like other dogs specially adapted to water retrieving, their coat is thick and curly, although some have longer, more wavy hair. Traditionally, the hindquarters are trimmed leaving a tassel on the end of the tail.

Left: Originally an African hunting dog and unknown beyond Central Africa until the 1870s, the Basenji is a curiosity on several counts. It is primarily distinguished as being the dog that has no bark - the result of an inherited condition of the larynx. Instead, it produces a kind of chuckle and can growl and whine. It is also sometimes called the Barkless Dog or Congo Terrier. Even more strange, perhaps, is this good-tempered dog's habit of cleaning itself with its tongue like a cat, and its ability to trot like a horse. The erect ears and wrinkled brow give the Basenji an alert intelligent air, and indeed it is an excellent all-round hunting dog, also used as a valuable tracker and watchdog in the African bush.

WINNER

Above: The Komondor's thick white coat falls right to the floor and the coarse hair is naturally corded into a mass of wavy ringlets. It needs careful grooming to bring it up to top- class show standard. A good brushing and combing daily will prevent it getting matted, but for the traditional corded look, wash the coat and allow it to dry without brushing.

Below: *Originally bred as a ratter, the Dandie Dinmont has found new popularity as an unusual and appealing pet. It has a low-slung, long body with a feathery tail, and the head looks almost as if it belonged to another dog: large and hairy with a bushy mop of hair and bright intelligent eyes. Brush the coat daily and clip it away from the eyes.*

Right: *With its thick curly coat, pear-shaped head and long, floppy ears, the Bedlington Terrier looks more like a little defenseless lamb than a hardy and enthusiastic hunter of rats, mice, foxes and badgers. Its coat is usually clipped and shaved to show off the whippetlike silhouette. Although loyal to its owners, the Bedlington Terrier has to be watched with other dogs, as the old fighting instinct comes out and it can be aggressive.*

Left: Like its name, the Pug is short, compact and could in no way be described as pretty. Nevertheless, with its stocky short-legged body, blunt, wrinkled face and curly pig's tail, it is very popular. No one is totally sure of its origins, but from many old paintings and china replicas, we know it has been a favorite for centuries. Although the dogs make intelligent and very playful pets, they do require a degree of devotion from their owners. The Pug can be difficult and unfriendly, especially with strangers; if warmth and diet are not strictly controlled, it is prone to colds and to gastric problems; and despite being short-coated, it needs regular vigorous brushing.

Right: When an ancient breed such as the Ibizan Hound remains little changed for thousands of years, recognizing it in ancient sketches and artefacts is sure to produce a shiver of excitement. This particular dog has been identified on a dish dating back to the Pharaohs (3100 to 2700BC) and was probably introduced to Ibiza from Egypt about 3,000 years ago. It has remained true to type mainly thanks to the remoteness of its Spanish island home, so that today it still looks very like Anubis, the Ancient Egyptian god of death. The Ibizan Hound has a lean greyhound profile, with a long, narrow head but rather large ears. Elegant but robust, it is an excellent hunter and retriever and loves being outdoors.

Above: The Chinese Crested, or Chinese Hairless, dog is said to be the original ancestor of the strangely soft-skinned and petite Mexican Hairless. Unlike that dog, the Chinese Crested does sport tufts of hair – on the tail, paws and, almost comically, around the face, in the form of long silky eyebrows and moustaches. It makes a fine pet, being affectionate and clean, extremely dainty, yet lively. The surprisingly warm, soft skin can be any range of delicate pastel colors, from a gray-blue to pink or gold or a combination of these shades. Curiously, the skin changes color during the year, being lighter in winter. Dating back to at least 1000BC, when it was common in China, the Chinese Crested is now extinct in that country, but is becoming more popular in the UK and North America.

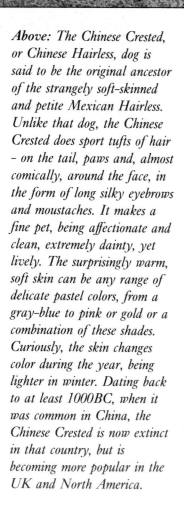

Dogs with a difference

Left: The distinctive Chow Chow is descended from the spitz family. With its thick woolly coat, broad head and collarlike ruff, it looks like a miniature lion padding along on small round catlike feet. However, it is not fierce, although it can be aloof and may threaten a stranger. The Chow Chow is a totally loyal pet and a useful guard dog, but not particularly easy to look after. It needs firm handling from an early age and is susceptible to a variety of illnesses, so keep it scrupulously clean. Brush the thick mane every day, but only bath the dog once a year.

Below: The stocky, hairy little Affenpinscher is sometimes called the Monkey Dog on account of its comical facial features. 'Affe' means monkey in German and 'pinscher' means terrier. The head is rounded, with shaggy hair almost hiding the black nose and lips and surrounding the deep round eyes. The dog is usually black, and has a lively yet obedient nature that has made it popular as a guard dog, as well as an entertaining pet and enthusiastic rabbit hunter. The Affenpinscher tends to lose its coat in a centrally heated home and will require special grooming.

Index

Index prepared by
Stuart Craik

123

Picture credits

The publishers wish to thank the following photographers and agencies for supplying photographs for this book. The photographers have been credited by page number and position on the page: (B) Bottom, (T) Top, (C) Center, (BL) Bottom Left, etc.

David Dalton: 10(CL), 14(T), 18(T), 19, 22(T), 25, 28(B), 30(B), 30-1(T), 31, 33(T), 34, 34-5(B), 36(B), 38, 39(B), 43(B), 47, 48(T), 50-1(B), 55(BL), 60(T), 61, 68, 70, 71, 74(B), 76(B), 80-1(T), 80(B), 81(B), 82(R), 85(BL), 86(T), 86-7(B), 88(T), 96(B), 99, 100(B), 105(L), 106, 107(BL), 110, 111, 113, 114, 115(T), 116, 117(B), 118, 121(BR)

C.M. Dixon: 10(T), 11(T,C,B)

Marc Henrie: Endpapers, 5, Title page, 8, 10(B), 12(T,B), 13, 14-15(B), 15, 16, 17, 18-19(B), 20, 21, 22(B), 23, 24, 26(T), 26-7(B), 27, 28(T), 28-9(B), 32, 33(B), 36(T), 37, 39(T), 40(T), 40-1(B), 41, 42, 43(T) 44, 48-9(B), 49, 50(T), 51, 52, 52-3(B), 53, 54, 55(T,BR), 56, 57, 58, 59, 60(B), 62-3(B), 63, 64, 65, 66-7, 67, 72, 73, 74(T), 75, 76(T), 77, 81(T), 82(L), 83, 85(BR), 87, 88(B), 89, 90, 91, 92, 93, 94, 95, 96(T), 97, 98, 100(T), 101, 102, 103, 104, 105(R), 107(T,BR), 108-9, 109, 112, 115(B), 117(T), 119, 120(TL), 120-1, 124

Frank Lane Picture Agency: 45(Silvestris), 46(Silvestris), 69(Silvestris), 78(Silvestris), 79(Silvestris), 84(Silvestris), 85(T, Roger Tidman)

Right: A beautiful Rough Collie takes time to pose for the camera. This breed makes an affectionate family pet and, despite appearances, that long silky coat is not too difficult to keep in good condition – as long as you brush it thoroughly every day. Rough Collies enjoy plenty of exercise, including free-ranging runs in open spaces.